The Sensational Skillet Cookbook

Create Spectacular Meals with Your Electric Skillet

WENDY LOUISE

OTHER BOOKS BY WENDY LOUISE

THE COMPLETE CROCKERY COOKBOOK: CREATE SPECTACULAR MEALS WITH YOUR
SLOW COOKER

RUSH HOUR RECIPES: RECIPES, TIPS AND WISDOM FOR EVERY DAY OF THE YEAR
(CO-AUTHORED WITH BROOK NOEL)

CHAMPION PRESS, LTD.
FREDONIA, WISCONSIN
Copyright © 2004 Wendy Louise

ISBN 1-891400-25-8
LCCN: 2004110035

Manufactured in the United States of America
10 9 8 7 6 5 4 3 2

Dedication

I would like to dedicate this book to the memory of my "Great Aunt" Betty, a fabulous cook in her day. And also to all the other good cooks in my family—I learned from the best!

A special thank you is expressed for Brook Noel and the staff at Champion Press Ltd.—with out you this book would have been only a dream.

And very special gratitude goes out to all my friends who shared their family recipes and favorite skillet-dishes for print in this book...your additions are wonderful!

Special thanks go out to Megan Meier and Chef Katy Keck of Bush's® Best Beans for sharing 3 delightful recipes from their creative kitchens (see pages 54 and 5, 126 and 7, 158 and 9).

Contents

Introduction

When I was first married (many, many years ago) my Great Aunt Betty, who worked for the Electric Company, gave me a wonderful wedding present—my first electric skillet. I was thrilled. Just as I used it then, it has remained one of my favorite cooking appliances today. Dependable, accurate, and user-friendly, with its convenient temperature-dial and non-stick surface it has remained a faithful cooking staple in my kitchen repertoire.

The electric skillet (or fry pan) is very versatile. I have used it to stir-fry, sauté and simmer. I have braised, 'broasted,' stewed and boiled with it. I have fried, grilled and even toasted. It has served me well for breakfast, lunch and dinner. I have deep fried and I have flambéed; I have used it as a food warmer on buffet tables; I have carried it to pot-lucks and plugged it back in. I've used it on the kitchen counter, at the table and at the cabin. Portable, storable and easy to clean—I'm not so sure I could live without it anymore!

I have cooked fancy foods and rustic foods, everyday family dinners and company-coming-for-dinner dinners. I have traded recipes and I have inherited recipes. I have replicated recipes from my travels, and I have invented a few new ones along the way.

The collection of recipes within these pages are meant to excite you to get out your electric skillet and start cooking—to start inventing and start creating your own recipes. Take what you like and leave the rest—there is something here to please all palates—and all palettes! So "fire up the pan" and tempt your taste buds and let's get started...

It should be noted, that the recipes in this book are generally written to serve 4 to 6 people, unless specifically noted. One can cook comfortably for 4 to 6 in an electric skillet, and sometimes up to 8, due to the limitations of the brand and make of the skillet, and the general size they come in. When cooking for more, I suggest adding a "Menu Stretcher" (see page 93) or a dish from the "Beyond the Pan" chapter (see pages 221-250) to extend your serving capabilities.

Wendy Louise

Getting Started...

Every recipe in this book includes 3 items: a bit of introductory esoteric information, the recipe itself, and a secret for success. By dividing the recipes in this manner, it is my hope that I can clearly explain the cooking process and flavor value for each recipe.

Cooking is not an exact science, but an art. Yes, we have measuring cups, and measuring spoons and weight scales—but we each bring our own personalities and taste preferences to the table. These recipes are meant to be "stepping stones" and "suggested guidelines" for you. If you like more garlic, add more garlic. If you prefer non-stick spray to olive oil, use the non-stick spray. Omit the meat and turn the recipe into a vegetarian medley. The sky is kind of the limit when it comes to cooking. Be inventive.

I come from a family that used a "hollow palm" of salt, as opposed to a tablespoon. My mother used a "dab" and a "dollop", a "dash" and a "pinch." During the war, if the recipe called for 2 eggs, she figured out how to stretch the recipe with 1 egg. If the recipe called for shallots, and she only had onions, she accommodated. Like my mother, my mother-in-law also "just knew" when something was done...cook it for 27 minutes? Well maybe it took 32...she just knew...And somehow, I have been lucky enough to retain their "hands on" tutelage.

In this day of no-carbs, low-carbs, no-fats, low-fats, polyunsaturated, reconstituted, skim verses whole, margarine verses butter, organic verses hot-house, farm-fed verses range-fed, poached verses fried, baked verses broiled, super-sized verses mega-sized, real verses synthetic, microwave verses convection, take-out verses staying-in...what is a person to do? The other day I was selecting an item at the grocery store and the wrapper said "includes real cheese"...well, as opposed to what?—that just floored me! And I could buy two for the price of one... What's that old saying... "We are what we eat"...

Precisely...all the more reason to pick up this cookbook and start cooking "real food" in real kitchens for real families. In this book I have included pages on sauces and pan gravies from scratch, so you can forego that 'can of soup' to flavor your meal. I have suggested fresh vegetables and sensible portions of meat. Switching to Olive oil or Canola oil and just a pat of butter for frying keeps dishes lighter and healthier, yet flavorful. Eating sensibly-sized entrees with the addition of a salad and vegetable balances out every meal. Adding a nice bread or a simple garnish takes it to one more step. It is my belief that eating satisfying and varied meals, remarkably prepared on a daily basis and in sensible portions, far out-weighs trying to stick to a lop-sided diet or convenience-food-schedule.

I include recommendations for using spices and cooking methods to gain depth of flavor and variety in your repertoire. I have rarely been a fan of the "one pot meal." I feel that foods need to be contrasted with combinations and textures, color and preparation—

warm verses cool, sweet complimented by salty or sour, lean and straight forward augmented by rich and gravy-ed. Some recipes use leftovers, some are quick and easy—others take time and a bit of practice. Over 165 recipes, an easy-to-refer-to index at the beginning of every chapter, a glossary of cooking terms and a temperature guide help you prepare interesting meals all year long. I think you will enjoy the diversity and convenience an electric skillet can bring to your kitchen.

In many recipes I have included serving suggestions or a reference to another dish that would make a good combination. The "Beyond the Pan" chapter offers non-cook dishes for assemblage while your main dish is cooking. A Secrets for Success index in the back, offers quick access to extra tips, tricks and safety suggestions referenced throughout the book.

When I set up my first kitchen, newly married and a novice at preparing meals I could barely boil water. Now I consider myself a very competent cook. Through failure and experimentation, and many calls home to my mother and mother-in-law I have gained a collection of "tried-and-trues"—my favorite recipes that have been now passed along to my daughter. Trading recipes and sharing cooking experiences with friends, have further complimented my skills—and now I pass them on to you.

A few final tips, before you start turning the pages and scanning the recipes. Read each recipe through before you try to cook it for the first time. Select the freshest ingredients possible and have them all within 'arms reach' as you start to cook. Be willing to substitute and re-arrange ingredients if needed to suit your family's tastes. Have all the tools necessary, i.e. tongs, paper toweling, small screw top jar, colander, etc. etc. Pay attention to detail and cook your meal with care. As I said before, cooking is an art—not an exact science. Creative cooking can be a rewarding experience. Mixing up an inventive meal in the comfort of your own kitchen can be far more relaxing and rewarding than "waiting in an exhaust-filled line at the drive-thru" or "picking a number and queuing up to the deli-counter"...not to mention the added savings to your pocketbook—at no expense to flavor.

Chapter One:
Every Day and Easy

Timeless and tasty
recipes to feed your family

Everyday and easy doesn't have to mean boring—same old, same old, again and again. This chapter is filled with family-style entrees that are filling, satisfying and great tasting.

From Southern Fried Chicken to Vegetarian Chili, from Chicken a la King to Pan Browned Pork Chops with Cranberry Sauce, you can make your daily menus varied and interesting.

Every Day and Easy Index

Aunty Mae's Southern Fried Chicken

I was introduced to this recipe more than 30 years ago and it still remains one of my favorite ways to cook chicken. Deeply golden brown, plain and simple, and oh so good—this recipe serves 4, at 2 pieces of chicken per person.

1 cut-up frying chicken
Water (for dipping chicken)
½ pie plate of flour
1 good palm's worth of salt
1 teaspoon baking powder
Crisco®
¼ cup butter

Mix flour, salt and baking powder together. Wet chicken pieces in water and then roll in pie plate of flour mixture, dredging each piece to coat evenly and well. Setting your electric skillet on a high setting (350 to 375 degrees), melt Crisco® to arrive at a ¼ -inch depth of hot oil. Add in butter to melt. Get oil hot enough so chicken bubbles in oil when you put pieces in pan. Brown chicken quickly on each side, turning once. Continue to fry, covered but vented, for 45 to 50 minutes, or until chicken is deep-golden brown, cooked through and juices run clear. After initial browning, turn heat down to a setting of 350 degrees. Turn chicken pieces every 10 to 15 minutes, always adding back cover slightly vented. If chicken is browning faster than you like, turn pan setting down to 325 degrees.

Secrets for Success:

The success of this recipe depends on getting the oil just to the right temperature before adding the chicken. The initial browning should be done at an oil temperature of 350 to 375 degrees. The oil should bubble when the chicken is placed in the pan. This prevents over-absorption of oil into the coating. **For example**: if the recipe calls for oil to be at 375 degrees, initially set the pan at 400 degrees to inhibit a drop in oil temperature when food is first added to the pan. If you need oil at 350 degrees, set the pan for 375, and so on. After a few minutes of quick-frying you can then adjust the temperature downward as needed to finish the dish. – **This is called the "shallow pan method for deep frying"—a method that will be used for other recipes in this book.**

For southern fried chicken put the largest pieces in first, adding legs and wings last, so the meatier pieces cook the longest. You do not want to over-crowd the pan! Trying to fry too much food in too little oil will decrease both the temperature and the cooking efficiency of the oil, causing a risk for greasy coating and soggy results.

The second secret for crisp chicken is to keep the cover slightly vented at all times.

The third secret to "southern fried chicken" is to leave the skin on—a must for this recipe.

Chicken Parmigiana

Fried up in the skillet till crusty and golden, covered with pasta sauce and melted cheese, this recipe makes a tasty and hearty dish for 4 (at 1 chicken breast piece per person).

4 boneless, skinless chicken breasts, pounded thin
½ pie plate of flour
1 egg, lightly beaten with 1 tablespoon water, in a shallow dish
½ pie plate dry bread crumbs (or Japanese bread crumbs)
A little olive oil
1 to 2 tablespoons butter
Tomato-based pasta sauce, your choice of brands
½ cup shredded mozzarella cheese
Parmesan cheese
Cooked pasta, at serving time

Pound chicken breasts to flatten. Dredge in pie plate of flour and then dip in beaten egg mixture. Roll in breadcrumbs to coat evenly and well. Heat olive oil and butter in your skillet on a medium-high heat setting to 350 degrees. Gently add chicken and sauté/fry on each side until golden brown. Turn down heat setting slightly and continue cooking until chicken is cooked through and juices run clear. (Cooking times will vary with thickness and size of the pounded meat.) Add a little more oil if necessary, to prevent sticking. Spread a coating of pasta sauce on top of each chicken piece. Top with mozzarella cheese and a sprinkle of Parmesan. Cover and continue cooking until all is hot and cheese is melt-y. Serve "as is" or on a bed of pasta. Add your favorite salad to complete the meal.

Secrets for Success:

Using a mixture of olive or cooking oil along with the butter keeps the butter from burning at high temperatures.

If you are dieting and are concerned about 'portion control' cut the pounded chicken breasts in half— extending the serving capability to 8 portions. Add a generous side of steamed broccoli with lemon wedges or a side of steamed fresh green beans to extend the dish. Plating your entrée (rather than serving 'family style') and adding steamed vegetables on the side is a great way to 'portion control' the amount you eat.

Chicken a la King

Old fashioned—yes. Comfort food—yes. My mother used to make this dish when I was little and I thought the toast points were 'soooo fancy'. Talk about a timeless dish! You can make it for one or make it for the whole family. It's still contemporary and it's still tasty and economical. This recipe makes 4 to 6 servings.

2 to 3 cups diced, cooked chicken (use canned or leftover from a previous meal)
¼ cup butter
¼ cup flour
1 cup milk
1 cup canned chicken broth
Salt and white pepper to taste
A splash of Sherry (optional)
1 small can mushrooms, drained
½ cup frozen peas, thawed (from a full package of peas)
4 to 6 patty shells or lightly-buttered toast or tube-style biscuits

Setting electric skillet on a medium heat setting, melt butter. Add flour to pan and blend, making what is called a "roux". Whisk in milk and then chicken broth, stirring all the while until the basic white sauce becomes thickened and smooth. (As a side note, white sauce is also known as Bechamel Sauce and when chicken broth is added to or substituted for the milk it becomes known as a Veloute Sauce.) Season lightly with salt and white pepper to taste. Add extra broth if needed to arrive at the thickness you prefer. Fold in cooked chicken, canned mushrooms and lastly the peas. Add optional Sherry for flavor and gently heat until all is warmed through. Serve over store-bought patty shells, buttered toast, tube-style biscuits (prepared to package instructions), or toast points (see directions below). Prepare the remainder of the package of peas as a side vegetable.

Secrets for Success:

Boil up the rest of the package of peas in a little water with 1 to 2 tablespoons of sugar and a sprig of mint (if you have it). Serve the **Sugared Peas** as your side dish.

Instead of leftover chicken or canned chicken, try deli chicken. On your way home pick up a Deli Roasted Chicken—what a convenient way to have cooked chicken for a recipe! And, as a bonus, the seasonings used on the deli-chicken will add extra flavor to your recipe.

Toast Points

Cut lightly buttered toast cross-wise from corner to corner to make triangles, and then cross-wise from the other corners, ending with 4 triangles. Arrange the triangles around a center piece of toast that has been left whole (and lightly buttered or not). Mound the A la King on the center piece of toast, so the 4 triangle-pieces peek out from underneath, forming "points." Garnish the dish with a sprig of parsley or 'architectural' sprigs of chive.

Chicken Marengo

Adventuresome in flavor—what a tasty dish to offer your family on a cold winter night in the middle of the week. This recipe serves 4 to 6.

1 cut-up frying chicken
Olive oil, to lightly cover bottom of pan
½ cup white wine, or cooking wine
1 to 2 mashed and minced cloves of garlic
1 pinch crushed thyme
1 bay leaf
1 to 2 tablespoons chopped parsley
1 cup canned chicken broth
1 medium-size can whole tomatoes, with juice
¼ cup butter
1 onion, thinly sliced
1 package sliced mushrooms (or you can use canned)
The juice from one lemon
1 small can pitted black olives, drained
A dash of cognac for taste (optional)
Cooked rice, at serving time

On a medium to high heat setting (350 degrees) sauté/fry chicken pieces in heated olive oil until nicely browned. Add next 6 ingredients to skillet. Break up tomatoes with a wooden spoon. Cover and reduce heat (250 to 300 degrees) simmering for about 30 to 40 minutes, or until chicken is tender and juices run clear. Remove chicken to warm platter. "Tent" platter with foil or hold chicken in 200-degree oven. Turn up heat setting in skillet to start reducing pan juices. Once pan juices have begun to reduce, melt in butter. Add sliced onion and mushrooms to cook. Add in lemon juice and add back chicken. Top with black olives. Sprinkle with a dash of cognac (optional) and cover. Continue cooking till all is warmed through and onion is tender. Serve over white or brown rice.

Secrets for Success:

The secret to this dish is the second cooking of the chicken to meld all the flavors. Those last few minutes glaze the chicken and bring all the flavors together. You'll think you are in the Mediterranean when you taste this dish. Serve it on a cold winter night along with some rustic bread and a nice salad.

For convenience I tend to use minute-style rice for my side dish. Both white and brown rice come in instant-style brands and easily cook-up in a few minutes, while you are finishing your entrée in the skillet.

Country Fried Chicken with Easy Pan Gravy

Just like my Aunt Louise used to make when she'd come to visit, this recipe serves 4 (at 2 pieces of chicken per person).

Fried Chicken:
1 cut-up frying chicken
1 egg, beaten with ¼ cup milk
½ pie plate of dry bread crumbs, or fine cracker crumbs, seasoned lightly with salt
Crisco®
1 to 2 tablespoons butter

Dip chicken pieces into egg-milk mixture and then dredge in bread crumb mixture, coating evenly and well. Melt Crisco® and butter into 375-degree pan, coating bottom of pan. Brown chicken pieces until golden, maintaining a temperature of 350 degrees. Turning down heat setting, cover tightly and continue to cook until chicken is tender and juices run clear, about 30 minutes. Uncover and cook 10 minutes more to re-crisp coating. Remove chicken to warm platter or oven and reserve until serving time. Continue in the same skillet to make gravy, utilizing the pan drippings.

Pan Gravy:
1½ cups milk, divided
3 tablespoons flour
½ teaspoon salt
Dash of pepper
Kitchen Bouquet® or Maggi® sauce, optional for additional flavor and color

Using a small screw-top jar, shake half of the milk with the flour and salt until mixed. Pour shaken mixture into pan drippings, (You need at least 2 to 3 tablespoons of drippings remaining in the skillet. Add more butter to the skillet if you need more drippings for base of gravy.) Continue to cook and whisk all the while on a medium-heat setting, getting up flavorful bits from bottom of pan. Add remaining milk. Continue to stir and heat until gravy becomes thickened and smooth. Add more milk if you feel you need to thin the gravy to a desired consistency. Season to taste with salt and pepper. Add a little Kitchen Bouquet® to enrich color and flavor if you wish. Drizzle a little gravy over chicken and serve the rest on the side with mashed potatoes.

Secrets for Success:
The secret to this recipe is the contrast of the crunchy chicken with the velvety, homemade gravy. So don't open a can of pre-made gravy!—whisk up your own, using the drippings in the skillet. Old fashioned Crisco® melted with a little butter fries up your chicken perfectly every time.

"Deep Fried" Shrimp

Succulent and tender, quick and easy, there is no reason not to cook deep fried shrimp at home. Count on about 6 to 8 large shrimp per person. Adjust the number according to the size of the shrimp you buy and your family's appetite.

1½ to 2 pounds large-count un-cooked shrimp (I like to use flash-frozen, shelled, de-veined shrimp with tails left on.)
½ pie plate of flour, seasoned lightly with salt and pepper
1 whole egg, beaten with 1 tablespoon of milk (or 1 egg white beaten stiff by itself)
½ pie plate of Japanese breading crumbs (or use finely crushed cracker crumbs)
Cooking oil (I like Canola oil)
Store bought shrimp-cocktail sauce, for serving or Homemade Tartar Sauce, for serving (see recipe to follow)

Thaw shrimp according to package instructions and pat dry. Dredge shrimp in seasoned flour to coat, shaking off any excess. Dip into beaten egg mixture (or beaten egg white) and then roll in breading crumbs to coat well. Heat a depth of ¼ to ½ -inch cooking oil to 375-degree temperature. Quickly "deep fry" the coated shrimp, using the "shallow pan frying method" (see page 17) until golden brown and shrimp are opaque, about 3 minutes on each side. Do not over cook or crowd pan, Remove shrimp with slotted spoon or tongs and drain on paper towels. Serve immediately with a spicy shrimp-cocktail sauce and/or homemade Tartar Sauce.

Secrets for Success:

Patting the shrimp dry and then dipping in flour makes the shrimp easier to coat with the following egg, then cracker crumbs. If you prefer not to use the whole egg, you can use just a beaten white, omitting the yolk and milk altogether. In today's market flash-frozen shrimp come already shelled and de-veined, tails left on—a very convenient alternative to buying fresh and cleaning yourself. Buy the large-count for meaty, beautiful shrimp. Thaw according to package instructions and make sure to pat dry before proceeding with recipe.

Homemade Tartar Sauce

1 cup mayonnaise (use low fat if you like)
1 tablespoon finely minced onion
1 tablespoon pickle relish (or finely chopped pickle)
1 to 2 teaspoons chopped capers
½ teaspoon Dijon-style mustard
A smidge of paprika
1 tablespoon finely chopped parsley
1 to 2 teaspoons fresh lemon juice

Mix all and refrigerate until serving time. Serve in individual bowls for dipping.—A good sauce for shrimp or fish!

Shrimp Tempura

Don't let the name Tempura scare you. Make it once and you'll be a pro. Use 6 large shrimp per person.

1½ to 2 pounds large-count un-cooked shrimp, shelled, de-veined, tails left on
2 eggs, separated
1 cup very cold water
1 cup flour
4 tablespoons cornstarch
A pinch of sugar
Canola oil or peanut oil
Serve with Homemade Dipping Sauce, or a sauce of your choice

To make tempura batter, whisk egg yolks with ice cold water in medium-size bowl. In separate bowl, mix together flour, cornstarch and sugar. Then gradually whisk flour mixture into cold egg mixture until smooth. Don't over work. Beat egg whites stiff and gently fold into batter. Again, don't over work batter. On a 400-degree setting bring a depth of ½ -inch oil to a temperature of 375 degrees. Pat thawed shrimp dry and dip into batter, coating evenly. Quickly "deep fry" the battered shrimp in hot oil until golden brown, about 3 minutes per side, using the "shallow pan frying method" (see page 17). Do not crowd when frying. Cook in batches if necessary. Carefully remove and drain on paper towels. Serve immediately with a favorite dipping sauce.

When frying shrimp, you need to maintain a high-oil temperature for quick-cooking efficiency. Do not crowd shrimp in skillet, cooking in batches if necessary. Serve the Tempura Shrimp immediately to prevent batter from becoming soggy. Add the sauce recipe below for a special treat.

Homemade Dipping Sauce

Bouillon or broth
Sherry (or sweet sake)
Soy sauce
Grated prepared horseradish, to taste
Grated fresh ginger root, to taste

Combine equal parts bouillon, Sherry (or sweet sake) and soy sauce to make base for sauce. Flavor to taste with prepared horseradish and grated fresh ginger. Serve in individual dipping bowls. Sauce will be thin. (Thicken with cornstarch if you wish.) Serve in little bowls for dipping. If you don't want to make your own sauce, buy several commercially-made dipping sauces from the Oriental section of your market. Have a taste-testing party to decide who likes what best.

"French Fried" Shrimp

Lightly battered, freshly made—French-fried shrimp plunged into chilled spicy sauce—is there anything better! Estimate 6 to 8 good sized shrimp per person.

1½ to 2 pounds large-count un-cooked shrimp, shelled, deveined, tails left on
1 cup flour
½ teaspoon salt
½ teaspoon sugar
1 egg, lightly beaten
1 cup very cold water
2 tablespoons vegetable oil
Canola oil
Serve with Homemade Zippy Dipping Sauce, or a sauce of your choice

Mix flour, salt and sugar together in a small bowl. In a separate, larger bowl whisk the beaten egg, cold water and vegetable oil until blended. Gradually whisk flour mixture into egg mixture until blended to form a smooth batter. Don't overwork batter. On a 400-degree setting bring ½ -inch depth of oil to 375 degrees. Pat thawed shrimp dry before dipping into batter to coat thoroughly. Cook quickly in the hot oil, about 3 minutes per side, until golden brown, using the "shallow pan frying method" (see page 17). Carefully remove and drain on paper towels. Serve shrimp immediately with your favorite cocktail sauce, or use the homemade recipe that follows.

Secrets for Success:

To successfully fry shrimp, make sure your oil is up to temperature for quick cooking and to eliminate the chance for soggy batter. If using frozen shrimp, thaw according to package instructions, being sure to pat dry before coating with batter. Do not crowd skillet, cooking in batches if needed. Drain the cooked shrimp on paper towels before serving.

Zippy Dipping Sauce

1 cup prepared, store-bought chili sauce
2 to 3 tablespoons fresh lemon juice
1 to 2 tablespoons finely-minced onion (to add taste, crunch and texture)
A dollop of prepared horseradish sauce
A dash of Worcestershire sauce
A dash of Tabasco® sauce
A dash of salt

Mix first 3 ingredients together to make base for sauce. Add last 4 ingredients according to taste. Chill until serving time. Serve in individual dipping bowls. Pass additional horseradish, Worcestershire and Tabasco® for each person to "doctor" their sauce to their liking.

Lucile's Round Steak Dinner

Newly wed and a novice cook, this was the first dinner that I cooked in my wedding present-electric skillet. Taught to me by my mother in law, it remains a favorite today—With fresh green beans, picked from the garden just like she did and her tender dumplings, this recipe makes 6 delicious servings.

1 ½ to 2 pounds round steak, ½ -inch thick, cut into serving
  pieces
½ pie plate of flour
Salt and pepper
Garlic powder
Oregano, crushed between your fingers
1 onion, sliced
Water
Fresh green beans, trimmed of ends and vein, left whole
A dash of cooking Sherry
2 to 3 tablespoons cooking oil
1 to 2 tablespoons butter
Serve with dumplings (see recipe page 34)

Lightly season dredging-flour with a little pepper, garlic powder and crushed oregano. Dredge serving-size round-steak pieces in flour mixture to coat evenly. Heat oil and butter in skillet and gently brown meat on both sides. Add sliced onion and about 2 cups of water. Season lightly with salt, pepper, garlic powder and oregano. Cover skillet and simmer for about 30 minutes. Add more water during cooking process if necessary. After 30 minutes add trimmed fresh green beans, cover and continue to simmer until meat is done and beans are just tender, about 10 to 15 minutes more. Flavor with a little Sherry to taste and adjust seasonings if necessary. Make dumpling dough (see dumpling recipe page 34) and drop onto stew. Cover and continue to cook until dumplings are shiny and set, about an additional 10-15 minutes. Total cooking time for entire recipe is about 1 hour or a little longer. Serve all with pan gravy that has resulted in the skillet. The dumplings will have automatically thickened the pan sauces nicely and no additional gravy will be needed.

Secrets for Success:

The beans make this recipe! Make sure you use fresh, whole green beans. Buy them from your market and use promptly—or better yet, pick them from your own garden while the meat is simmering! Add beans last half of cooking time to avoid over-cooking. Homemade dumplings add a fabulous touch to this dish.

Lucile's Dumplings

2 cups flour
4 teaspoons baking powder
½ teaspoon of salt
A pinch of oregano, crushed between your fingers
1 cup milk

In a mixing bowl (using a wooden spoon or a fork) mix dry ingredients together and then add milk, mixing until soft-dough is formed. Don't overwork dough. (You want your dumplings to be light and tender, not tough and chewy.) Drop by rounded teaspoons-full onto your simmering stew during last 15 minutes of cooking time. Cover and continue cooking until dumplings are shiny and set.

Secrets for Success:

Do not over-mix nor over-work dumpling batter. Form your dumplings small and uniform in size to allow for consistent cooking and light, spongy results. Too large of dumplings tend to get gummy, while taking too long to cook and absorbing too much moisture from the simmering dish. **Bonus Recipe:** This dumpling recipe may be used as a wonderful side-dish for other meals by just omitting the oregano to make a basic batter. While your dinner is cooking, in a separate pot of boiling salted water, cook basic dumplings covered for about 10 to 15 minutes. The dumplings will float to the top when done. Drain and toss with melted butter, or top with Brown Butter (see page 191). Serve the buttered dumplings in little side dishes, instead of potatoes, rice or noodles the next time you want to vary your menu!

Lorraine's Swiss Steak

When I was compiling recipes for this book I asked friends for their favorites—remembered from childhood. There is magic involved with the memories of what our mothers used to cook and this recipe makes 4 to 6 delicious servings.

1½ to 2 pounds round steak, ½-inch thick, cut into serving size pieces
2 to 3 tablespoons cooking oil
1 to 2 tablespoons butter
1 onion, sliced thin or chopped
1 to 2 green bell peppers, sliced into strips or chopped
1 to 2 (16 ounce) cans stewed tomatoes, un-drained
Salt and pepper to taste

Preheat electric skillet to 350 degrees with cooking oil and butter to cover bottom of pan. Cut round steak into serving-size pieces. Brown meat on both sides, then remove from pan. Sauté/fry onion and bell peppers in pan till slightly limp and glazed. Add meat back to pan. Pour on first can of stewed tomatoes, including liquid. Cover and reduce heat setting to a medium–simmer. Cook until meat is tender and flavors have melded, approximately 30 to 40 minutes. While steak is cooking add more stewed tomatoes if necessary, to arrive at the amount of sauce that you like. Adjust seasoning with salt and pepper to taste. Serve with mashed potatoes and the sauce "as is" from the pan.

Secrets for Success:

The secret to Lorraine's recipe is its simplicity. Don't "doctor it up" with extra spices—don't "mess" with the sauce—don't hesitate to have it become a family favorite! The wonderful flavor comes from the initial browning of the meat and then the browning of the onion and peppers before you start the simmering process with the tomatoes.

Spanish Beef and Rice

Quick to fix, easy to eat; written for a family of 4.

1 pound lean ground beef
½ cup chopped red onion
Cooking oil
1 teaspoon salt
½ teaspoon pepper
1 teaspoon chili powder
Dash cayenne
1 to 2 vine ripened tomatoes, seeded and diced
1 can yellow corn, drained
1 can bouillon or beef broth
1 green bell pepper, seeded and sliced in thin strips
1½ cups minute-style rice
1 or 2 green onions, sliced (including tops) for garnish

On medium to high heat setting, with 1 or 2 tablespoons of cooking oil, sauté ground beef and onion until beef is browned and onion is soft. Add the 4 seasonings, stir and cook 1 minute more. Add diced tomato, drained corn and bouillon. Bring to a boil. Stir in bell pepper strips and quick-cooking rice. Cover tightly and turn off heat. Cover and let stand for 5 minutes. Fluff with a fork before serving. Garnish with sliced green onion.

Secrets for Success:

Using a lean cut of ground beef and quick-cooking rice makes this a super-easy dish to prepare on a busy night in the middle of the week. Serve with a refreshing fruit salad for contrast, (see suggestions on pages 234 and 5 in the Beyond the Pan Section).

Soy-Sauce Beef with Broccoli

Beef and broccoli are definite "go-togethers." This recipe cooks up quickly to make 4 to 6 tasty servings.

1 to 1½ pounds beef sirloin, sliced into thin, stir-fry-size strips
Canola oil, just to cover bottom of pan
1 bunch fresh broccoli, trimmed to flowerets
2 to 3 green onions, sliced into julienne strips, including green
   tops (To julienne, means to cut into 'match-stick-like strips.)
2 tablespoons cornstarch
1 (14.5 ounce) can of beef broth
1 to 2 tablespoons of soy sauce, or to taste (or use a light-salt
   variety if you wish)
½ to 1 teaspoon of crushed red pepper flakes, or to taste
Cooked white or brown rice, or *cellophane noodles, at serving
   time.

Slice beef into very thin slices for quick cooking. Set heat setting at 350 degrees. In heated oil to cover bottom of pan, sauté/fry beef strips in batches, browning quickly as if you are stir-frying. Do not over cook and do not crowd. Remove meat from pan and set aside. Reduce heat setting to a medium temperature. Add more oil if necessary and stir-fry broccoli and green onions until tender-crisp. Using a small screw top jar, shake cornstarch with a small portion of canned beef broth until mixed. Set aside. Pour remaining broth into small bowl, adding soy sauce and red pepper flakes. Add shaken cornstarch mixture to bowl and blend well. Pour blended-broth mixture over broccoli and onions in the pan and bring to a boil, stirring until sauce becomes thickened and heated through. Return beef back to pan and stir just till heated. Do not over cook. Serve alongside white or brown rice, or *cellophane noodles.

Secrets for Success:

The secret to this recipe is not to overcook the ingredients! You want your meat to be tender and the broccoli to be tender-crisp. Over-cooking will turn everything to more like a stew than a stir-fry.

Cellophane Noodles provide a quick, easy side-dish-alternative to everyday rice. You can find them in the Oriental section of your grocery store. Try them out, if you haven't already done so. Prepare the noodles according to package instructions and serve alongside your stir-fry.

Aunty Joan's Chop Suey

Cooked until crunchy-tender, quick and delicious, this version of chop suey uses commonly found ingredients to serve a family of 4 to 6 and is a great way to get everyone to eat their veggies.

1 to 1½ pounds beef sirloin, cut into very thin (stir-fry size) strips
2 to 3 tablespoons cooking oil (*Canola or peanut oil)
1 cup diced celery
1 onion, diced
Canned mushrooms (*see mushroom note below)
1 tablespoon molasses
1 can beef broth
2 tablespoons cornstarch mixed with 3 tablespoons water in small jar
2 cups bean sprouts
1 small can water chestnuts, sliced very thin
½ teaspoon salt
Dash of pepper
2 tablespoons soy sauce
Cooked rice, at serving time (brown or white)
Crunchy chow mien noodles, for garnish (optional)
Chopped green onion tops, for garnish (optional)
Soy sauce, to pass at serving time

On 350-degree heat setting, in hot oil to cover bottom of pan, brown beef strips quickly (in batches if necessary). Do not over cook. Remove from pan and set aside. To the pan add diced celery and onion, mushrooms, molasses and beef broth. Turn down heat setting and simmer vegetables for 5 to 6 minutes. Add cornstarch mixture to pan and stir to thicken. Fold in bean sprouts and water chestnuts. Return beef strips to pan and heat through.

Do not over cook—you want your bean sprouts and water chestnuts to remain crunchy-crisp. Lightly season with salt, pepper and soy sauce to taste. Serve with cooked rice, garnishes of crunchy chow mien noodles and chopped green scallions, and a bottle of soy sauce to pass around on the side.

Secrets for Success:

*For browning meats in hot oil at high temperature, I suggest using Canola® oil, as it withstands high heat very well. Peanut oil is the best, but many people have allergies to peanuts, so use wisely. Brown meat in batches, to avoid overcrowding and improper browning.

*For a fun variation to this recipe, add a can of the cute little Oriental straw mushrooms. Usually you can find these in the Oriental or specialty-foods section of your grocery store. If using these delicate mushrooms, fold them in when you add the bean sprouts and water chestnuts. Be sure to drain and rinse thoroughly before using. (Sometimes you can be lucky enough to find fresh straw mushrooms in the produce department—use these delicate mushrooms if available for an exotic treat.)

Mr. Bieber's Egg Foo Yong ("Chinese Pancakes")

Many years ago when I was up at the cabin, my summering neighbor stopped in for a visit and we started trading recipes. In exchange for my stir-fry I received this wonderful recipe. Egg Foo Yong makes a great entrée for a light and satisfying dinner, or can be used as a side dish as well. Serve with a pot of green tea or tall glasses of iced-green tea, depending on the season. This recipe makes a bunch.

1 cup diced or shredded cooked chicken (Reserve stock if you've just cooked-up the chicken. It can be used in place of canned broth called for in homemade brown sauce.)
1 small onion, diced fine
1 small can water chestnuts, drained and sliced into little strips
Bean sprouts, sliced
6 eggs, beaten
Cooking oil, to cover bottom of pan
Chopped green onions (including tops) for garnish
Soy sauce, at serving time
Brown Sauce, at serving time

On 350-degree setting, heat cooking oil to cover bottom of pan. Mix first 4 ingredients into beaten eggs, blending well. As if you were making pancakes, spoon egg mixture into pan, making approximately 3-inch across and ½ - inch thick patties. Gently brown first sides until set. Turn once and brown second sides. The edges of the "pancakes" will get a little crispy and the pancakes themselves will remain soft but firm. (That's just the way you want them.) As they are done, remove to warm platter and tent with foil, or hold in 200-degree oven till all are done. Garnish with chopped green onion and serve with a bottle of soy sauce on the side. Add Homemade Brown Sauce to complete the dish.

Homemade Brown Sauce

2 cups canned chicken broth (or reserved chicken stock if you
   have it)
2 tablespoons cornstarch
2 tablespoons soy sauce

Once all "pancakes" have been cooked and reserved, make brown sauce in the same pan. In screw-top jar, shake cornstarch with ¼ cup broth (or stock) to mix. Set aside. Pour remaining broth (or stock) into skillet and bring to simmer. Add shaken-cornstarch mixture and stir until heated through and sauce has thickened. Stir in soy sauce to taste. Serve sauce warm, drizzled over Egg Foo Yong.

Secrets for Success:
My "culinary-savvy" neighbor divulged that he used his wife's crochet hoops to mold his Egg Foo Yung—thus keeping them from spreading one into the next! To this day I laugh at his ingenuity, although I never adopted his technique.

Making Pan Sauces and Gravies

Secrets for making successful pan sauces and gravies:

When using cornstarch to thicken a sauce, never add it directly into the sauce. Always dissolve it first in a little water, broth or wine and you will be guaranteed a smooth, lump-free sauce every time. Shaking it together with a little liquid in a screw-top jar works really well for this. Then gently blend the cornstarch mixture into the pan juices, stirring all the while till thickened. Stir in additional liquid to arrive at the consistency you desire. Season your sauce to taste at end of the cooking process.

The same principle works equally well when using flour to thicken gravy. Shake it up first with a little water or broth in a screw top jar. Then slowly whisk the shaken mixture into the pan juices, blending well. Continue to cook and add more liquid until your gravy arrives at the thickness and consistency that you like. Lastly season to taste with a little salt and pepper. You can also add a little Kitchen Bouquet®, Sauce Robert® or Maggi® for additional flavor and color if you wish.

Another secret to great-tasting sauce and/or gravy is to 'deglaze' your pan as a first step. Skim or drain off any excess oils or fats and discard. Over medium to high heat 'reduce' the remaining liquid in the pan—forming a condensed base for your sauce or gravy. Stirring all the while capture the flavorful bits from the bottom of the pan for extra flavor. You are now ready to proceed with your thickener and additional liquids.—So why open a can when you can make your own in minutes!

At the last minute "finish" the sauce or gravy with 1 pat of butter swirled in at the very end of cooking. This little detail adds depth and gloss and enriched flavor to the final product—and you will be oh so happy, you added this little "French touch."

Secrets for Success:

When making sauces and gravies, stick to these simple rules and you'll have great results every time. I also cannot stress enough, how important a little dash of Kitchen Bouquet®, Sauce Robert® or Maggi® can be for enriching additional flavor and color into your sauce. These condensed-flavor-seasonings are great to use in place of wine. They can usually be found in the spice section or gourmet aisle of your favorite market.

Pan Browned Pork Chops Glazed with Cranberry Sauce

Often overlooked, cranberry sauce goes with more than just turkey and the Holidays. Try this delicious recipe any season of the year, at 1 pork chop per person.

4 (½-inch thick) loin cut, pork chops, trimmed of excess fat
½ teaspoon black pepper
½ teaspoon dried sage, crushed between your fingers
2 tablespoons cooking oil
1 tablespoon butter
½ cup water
1 can whole-berry cranberry sauce
1 medium onion, diced
Mashed potatoes, buttered noodles, or homemade dumplings,
   at serving time

Trim any excess fat off pork chops. Rub pepper and sage into chops. Brown chops quickly on each side, "searing" to seal in juices, in 350-degree oil and butter. Lower heat setting and pour water into pan. Cover tightly and simmer about 15 minutes. Add more water as needed. Turn chops. Mix cranberry sauce and diced onion. Pour over chops. Cover again and continue to cook about 15 to 20 minutes more, until chops are done and flavors in sauce have melded. Serve with mashed potatoes, lightly buttered egg noodles or homemade dumplings. (If you are concerned about egg yolks in the egg noodles, try a No Yolk®-style noodle.)

Secrets for Success:

When using dried spices (such as the sage called for in this recipe) crush the spices between your fingers to release extra flavor before adding to the skillet.

*A side note about cooking pork chops: Do not over-cook pork chops, as they will become tough and dry. Meat that has been trimmed of excess fat will cook faster and dry-out quicker than untrimmed meat. By first searing (quickly browning at high temperature) lean meats on all sides, and even the edges, you contain the juices in the meat—helping to prevent drying out during further cooking. An acceptable temperature for doneness of pork is 160 degrees. By the time you've boiled and mashed your potatoes, or cooked and drained your noodles or dumplings, the chops will be done (or near to done) and all will be ready to serve.

Mom's Stuffed Pork Chops

My Mom had a way of taking the simplest of ingredients and making them into a sensational dish. A little stuffing, a special cut of pork chops (1 per person), a dash of spices, some pan gravy and voila!—a hearty dinner was served.

4 loin-cut pork chops, double-cut to 1 1/4 -inches thick (allow 1 chop per person)
Pepperidge Farm ® stuffing-croutons (or make your own, see recipe that follows)
2 to 3 tablespoons cooking oil
1 tablespoon butter
A pinch of dried oregano, crushed between your fingers
Water or apple juice, divided
Salt and pepper to taste

Slicing chops horizontally, carefully cut a pocket into middle of each chop, almost as if you are "butter-flying" the chops. Pack the pockets with your stuffing-croutons of choice and secure edges of chops with toothpicks to hold in stuffing. In hot oil and butter (350 degrees), brown stuffed chops quickly on both sides. Then sprinkle with crushed oregano. Add water or apple juice to pan. Lower heat-setting. Cover and simmer 20 to 25 minutes. Turn chops and add more water or apple juice as necessary. Cover and simmer for 20 to 25 minutes more, or until chops are done to your liking. Remove chops to warm platter and hold "tented" with foil, or hold in 200-degree oven. While chops are holding, make gravy from pan juices. In a small screw-top jar mix a little flour and water. Shake to blend well. Pour into skillet juices and stir, getting up all the flavorful bits from bottom of skillet. Stirring all the while, add additional water or apple juice until you arrive at desired thickened consistency. Lightly season gravy with salt and pepper to taste. Bring gravy to the table in warmed bowl or "sauce boat" and pass on the side, to drizzle over chops. Make sure to remove toothpicks from chops before serving.

Secrets for Success:

For convenience, have your butcher precut the pockets in the chops for you! Also, rather than buying a big package of pre-made stuffing—try making your own from the recipe below. Forego the mashed potatoes tonight because you have tasty stuffing instead. Add a favorite salad and warmed dinner rolls to complete the meal.

Make-Your-Own-Stuffing

1 slice of bread per chop, cubed, crusts removed if you like
A little minced onion or shallot
A dash of parsley
A dash of poultry seasoning
Butter

Simply sauté bread cubes along with seasonings and a little butter until lightly browned. Stuff chops just prior to cooking. **[Note:** Salad croutons can be made the same way, using non-stick cooking spray (or less butter) or by sautéing in a dry pan, with your choice of spices.**]**

Pork Chops a la Aunt Louise

My elderly Aunt (and middle namesake) had a farm in Indiana and I have a feeling they butchered their own pork and picked their own apples. A simple soul, she sure knew how to cook. From cast iron skillet on a wood-burning farm stove, to the later convenience of an electric skillet, she would have a tasty mid-day meal waiting for her farm hands...

¾-inch to 1-inch thick pork chops, trimmed of excess fat,
  (allow 1 per person)
A little salt and pepper
2 to 3 tablespoons cooking oil
1 tablespoon butter
Water or apple juice
Tart cooking apples, cored, peeled and sliced into fairly thick
  rings

Brown chops quickly on both sides (and the edge) in hot oil and butter. Season lightly with salt and pepper. Add a little water or apple juice and cover tightly. Reduce heat setting and simmer chops slowly until done, about 40 minutes. Turn chops halfway through and add more water or apple juice as necessary. Remove chops to warm platter and "tent" with foil to keep warm—or hold in 200-degree oven. Add apple slices to pan drippings and sauté just until warmed through, tender and glazed. Pour cooked apple slices, and any sauce, over reserved pork chops and serve immediately. Pass dinner rolls and a simple vegetable-side dish to complete the meal.

Secrets for Success:

Use good, tart cooking apples, such as Granny Smith, Pippin or McIntosh and make your slices 1/3 to 1/2-inch thick. Don't over cook or the slices will turn to mush. For this dish you want tender slices of warmed apple still holding their shape—not apple sauce!

MaryAnn's Peanut Butter Pork Chops

An inventive dish, adding yet more variety to the common pork chop...

4 large lean pork chops, (allow 1 per person)
Shortening
4 thick onion slices
¼ cup peanut butter
½ (10.5 –ounce) can condensed mushroom soup
¼ cup milk
1 teaspoon Worcestershire sauce
1 teaspoon salt (or to taste)
1/8 teaspoon pepper

Bring a small amount of shortening up to temperature and quickly brown pork chops on both sides. After browning, pour off excess shortening from skillet. Place a thick onion slice on top of each chop. Mix together remaining ingredients and pour over chops. Cover skillet, reduce heat setting, and simmer slowly for 45 minutes, or until chops are tender and cooked through.

Secrets for Success:

Initial browning and then slow simmering, keeps these chops succulent and tender. MaryAnn's delightful combination of peanut butter and onion makes for a dish suitable for everyday or company!—sometimes "old fashioned, 'down-home' goodness" is just what we want when company comes for dinner... Rather than entertaining your guests in the dining room...set your table in the kitchen for a cozy and comfortable, casual approach! We don't always have to have the formality of a dining room to entertain our guests. You'll be surprised at how relaxed your guests will be and how the conversation will flow, in such a casual setting. It's amazing how "good friends always end up around the kitchen table!"

Bush's® 3-Bean Chili

This tasty recipe is offered by Megan Meyer through the courtesy of the kitchens of Bush Brothers & Company. The combination of 3 varieties of Bush's Best® beans really makes the dish! This recipe makes 8 to 10 servings, so if you are a small family you might want to plan several meals around it (see suggestions to follow) or cut the recipe in half.

2 pounds lean ground round beef
3 teaspoons chili powder
1 small yellow onion, chopped
1 small green pepper, chopped
2 (16 ounce) cans BUSH'S Best® Dark Red Kidney Beans
2 (16 ounce) cans BUSH'S Best® Pinto Beans
2 (15 ounce) cans BUSH'S Best® Black Beans
1 (14.5 ounce) can tomatoes
1 (6 ounce) can tomato paste
1½ teaspoons salt
1 teaspoon garlic salt
½ teaspoon ground pepper
½ teaspoon cumin
Pinch of cinnamon, or to taste
Sour Cream, for garnish at serving time

On a medium to high heat setting brown ground beef, adding chili powder during browning process and mixing well. Add onion and green pepper to browned meat and continue browning for 2 minutes more. Drain off any excess fat. Stir in remaining ingredients except sour cream. Lower heat setting and simmer for at least 10 minutes to meld flavors. Top each bowl of chili with a dollop of sour cream at serving time.

Secrets for Success:

Here are 3 suggestions for additional meals. Enjoy!

Freeze half for an already-made-dinner when you need it. Cool the chili you are going to freeze. Place in an airtight container, date and freeze. Pull it out the night before, or the morning of, the day you want to serve it. Let it thaw in the refrigerator while you are at work and it will be ready to re-warm when you get home. Serve with a loaf of freshly warmed French bread and store-bought honey butter or bake up a quick batch of corn bread from a boxed mix. Freshen up your garnishes of sour cream and cheese to pass on the side.

Make an extra dinner by serving the re-warmed chili on top of hot, freshly baked potatoes. Garnish with shredded Cheddar cheese, sour cream and a snippet of chives.

Wrap leftover chili in soft tacos, top with shredded Cheddar cheese and warm in oven or microwave. Garnish with sour cream and/or guacamole and freshly chopped green onion.

Vegetarian Chili

A vegetarian dish, this "chili" gets its protein from the addition of the beans. Recipe written to serve 6.

1 red onion, diced
1 poblano or jalapeño chili pepper, seeded and diced fine
2 garlic cloves, or to taste, mashed and minced
1 teaspoon cayenne, or to taste
2 teaspoons chili powder, or to taste
1 red bell pepper, seeded and chopped
1 yellow bell pepper, seeded and chopped
1 green bell pepper, seeded and chopped
2 to 3 young zucchini, cut into bite-size disks, skin left on
2 ribs of celery, sliced
1 (15 ounce) can black beans, rinsed and drained well
1 (16 ounce) can garbanzo beans, rinsed and drained well
2 to 4 fresh tomatoes, chopped (or you can use canned)
1 can yellow corn, drained
1 can pitted black olives, drained
Olive oil

In a little olive oil, on medium to high heat setting, sauté/fry ingredients, adding them to skillet in order listed. Start with onion and end with corn and black olives. When all has been added, cook-down until tender, warm and sauce-y but vegetables still hold their shape—about 10 to 15 minutes. Do not over cook. Serve over cooked white rice, brown rice or macaroni. Garnish with shredded Cheddar cheese, sour cream and chopped fresh cilantro. Or, for a garnish-variation try this buttery-smooth Avocado Sauce:

Smooth Avocado Sauce

1 large or 2 medium ripe avocados, peeled and pitted
½ cup water
1 to 2 tablespoons juice from a fresh lemon or lime
1 garlic clove, mashed
Sea salt and white pepper, to taste

Blend all on high speed in blender or food processor until very smooth. Adjust seasonings to taste and serve immediately.

Secrets for Success:

When handling and seeding hot chili peppers (such as the jalapeño used in this vegetarian dish) use rubber gloves or wash your hands thoroughly when done. Be sure not to rub your eyes before you wash your hands!

Lori's Almost Vegetarian Zucchini Alfonse

Zucchini and avocado—a match made in heaven! Light, but rich, this recipe serves 6 along with a nice salad and bread.

4 medium to large zucchini
½ pie plate flour
Salt and pepper
Olive oil for cooking, plus 2 tablespoons more
1 package spaghetti sauce mix, to taste
1 (8 ounce) can tomato sauce
1 cup shredded mozzarella cheese
3 tablespoons grated Parmesan
1 ripe avocado, peeled, pitted and sliced at time of serving
Bacon, cooked crisp and broken into bite-size pieces (*see suggested microwave cooking method on next page)

Cut zucchini in half length-wise and then each half into 3 flat slices, ending with 6 long slices per zucchini. Lightly season flour with salt and pepper. Dredge slices in seasoned flour, shaking off any excess. Using a medium to high heat setting and olive oil to cover bottom of pan, fry zucchini in 4 batches until golden brown and tender. Add more olive oil as needed. Do not over crowd pan. Set batches aside on paper towels. Turn down heat setting. Add 2 more tablespoons olive oil, tomato sauce and spaghetti sauce mix to pan. Stir together and simmer 1 or 2 minutes to make sauce. Add back the zucchini slices into the sauce. Top with shredded mozzarella cheese. Cover and cook gently until cheese melts and all is heated through. Do not over cook. Uncover and arrange avocado slices onto the sauce-y zucchini. Top with crisped bacon and serve. Add a tossed salad and French bread to complete the meal.

Secrets for Success:

This dish is meant to be delicately seasoned, subtle in flavor and not drowning in sauce. The zucchini slices should be golden and tender but still hold their shape. **Vegetarian Note:** You will see that, throughout the book, I have included numerous recipes that can be easily transformed into vegetarian dishes. Although, I love nothing better than a good steak, I also enjoy serving meatless (or very light on the meat) dinners, from time to time.

Microwave Bacon

Standard-cut bacon (not too thick, not too thin)
Paper toweling
Microwave-safe plate or paper plate

A convenient way to make crisp, rendered bacon is to cook it in the microwave on paper toweling. Place bacon strips on several layers of paper toweling, on a paper plate. 4 strips of bacon usually need to cook about 4 minutes on high; 6 pieces for 6 minutes on high. (Cooking time is approximate due to variances in microwaves and thickness of bacon.) When bacon has crisped to your liking remove from microwave. Throw away the paper towels! Throw away the paper plate! Throw away the grease! Your bacon is now ready to crumble and use in a recipe.

Meat Meets Mac' for a One-Pot Dinner

Tasty, filling and all the convenience of a one-pot dinner...I always estimate 1 pound of beef for 4 servings.

1 pound lean ground beef
1 to 2 tablespoons cooking oil
¼ cup diced onion
2 tablespoons minced fresh parsley
1 (6-ounce) can tomato paste
1 cup canned, stewed tomatoes
2 cups water
½ teaspoon salt
1 teaspoon chili powder, or to taste (optional)
1 (8-ounce) package macaroni, uncooked
1 (15-ounce) can yellow corn, drained
Shredded Cheddar cheese (optional)
Sour cream (optional)

On a high heat setting, quickly brown beef in cooking oil. Spoon-off excess fat from skillet. Add next seven ingredients (onion through chili powder) and bring to a boil. Stir in macaroni. Cover, lower heat setting, and simmer 20 to 25 minutes. Add in corn and continue to simmer until macaroni is fully cooked and tender—another 5 to 10 minutes. Turn skillet down to warm setting and serve straight from the skillet. Serve as is, or top each serving with shredded Cheddar cheese and a dollop of sour cream.

Secrets for Success:

Variations Galore:

This is such a versatile dish. You can add and delete spices and ingredients to suit your family's tastes. For example, add some diced green pepper and substitute Mexican-style tomatoes for a Tex-Mex touch.

Or omit the corn and chili powder; add in a can of mushrooms and have a traditional "spaghetti-flavored" dish.

Change the style of the dish with different shapes and colors of pasta (using what you have on hand in your pantry—adjusting the cooking time for the different pastas used). You can even omit the beef and fold in diced, cooked chicken, canned tuna, or leftover meat toward the end of cooking.

And lastly, you could go completely vegetarian!—omitting the meat altogether, and sautéing-in a couple of sun-ripened tomatoes and/or garden-fresh zucchini, and then proceeding with recipe—maybe stirring in pitted-black olives instead of corn! Stirring in some sour cream (at end of cooking) would make a creamier (kind of stroganoff-style) dish. Experiment with melting different cheeses on top during last 5 minutes of cooking—or just sprinkling them on as a garnish at time of serving.

One basic recipe can take on many personalities, with a creative touch added by you! Suddenly meat, or no meat, meets more than just mac'!

Charlotte's Quick-Skillet Chicken and Rice Scramble

One skillet—one complete meal—how savvy is that!

1 pound chicken breast meat or chicken tenders, cut into bite size pieces
2 tablespoons Canola oil, divided
2 cups water or chicken broth
2 cups instant cooking rice (use white or brown, your choice)
1 cup yellow corn, green peas, or mixed vegetables (thawed)
1 to 2 teaspoons of mixed-seasoning-salt (such as Season-All® or Mrs. Dash®)
2 eggs, beaten for scrambling
2 green onions (with tops), diced

On a medium-high to high heat setting, quickly brown chicken bites in 1 tablespoon hot oil. Add water and seasonings, stirring to mix. Fold in rice and your choice of vegetable. Turn down heat setting, cover and cook gently for 15 minutes, or until rice is fluffy, liquid has been absorbed, and chicken is done. Move chicken/rice mixture to side of skillet, making room to scramble eggs. Turn heat setting back up slightly. Add beaten eggs to emptied part of skillet and gently scramble in the remaining tablespoon of oil. When eggs are done, break them up, and incorporate the two mixtures together. Top with a garnish of diced green onion. While dinner is cooking bake a batch of box-mix blueberry muffins to serve with the meal.

Secrets for Success:

Never under estimate the Nanny, when she needs to cook up a quick, nutritious family favorite! Be sure not to over-cook the eggs—they should be tender and softly set—not tough and rubbery. Also, be careful not to cook eggs at too high of a heat setting, as this will lead to tough and chewy eggs as well.

Ham and Broccoli Roll Ups with Mustard Sauce

A great way to get your family to eat a healthy veggie—this recipe makes 6 servings.

6 spears fresh broccoli, cooked al dente and drained
6 thin slices deli-Swiss cheese
6 thin slices deli-ham
1 tablespoon butter
2 tablespoons flour
2 teaspoons Dijon-style mustard
1½ cups milk
Salt and white pepper
¼ cup grated Parmesan cheese
Paprika
Cooked rice or rice pilaf, at serving time

Roll a slice of Swiss cheese around each cooked broccoli spear. Then roll each with a slice of ham. Set aside. In your skillet, on medium heat setting, make a roux (i.e. thickening paste for your sauce) by first melting the butter and then adding in the flour, stirring with a whisk. Gently blend in mustard and milk, stirring to mix. Stir and cook until sauce thickens and is heated through. Lightly season with salt and white pepper. Blend in grated Parmesan. Add roll-ups to sauce. Sprinkle with a dusting of paprika. Cover and gently simmer till all is heated through. Serve as a light entrée with cooked rice (of your choice) on the side and a favorite salad (see Beyond the Pan Section for ideas) to complete the meal.

Secrets for Success:

When making your basic white sauce use white pepper for a sophisticated touch.

A side note on white based sauces: Why use a can of commercial cream soup when you can easily make your own creamy sauce in minutes..."Homemade" is so much healthier and better in flavor than that can of processed soup. You can add just the flavorings you desire, as in this case Dijon mustard and Parmesan, also arriving at the consistency you prefer. So put away the can opener, forego the goopy soup, and make your own silken sauce...the results are so satisfying, and far easier than fussing with a can opener and that pesky lid that just won't open!

A side note on broccoli: Buy the freshest, firmest, greenest broccoli you can find. Cut off the tough bottoms of the stalks (about an inch or so) and trim off the little side leaves too. Steam covered in a colander over 1 inch of boiling water just until al dente (crisp tender). Drain under cold water to stop the cooking process if not using immediately. Your broccoli is now *ready to use in a recipe.*

Making White Sauces

Every cook should know how to make this most basic of sauces (also referred to in French cooking as the Mother Sauce). So I thought I would include a page or two, a primer if you will, on how to make this versatile sauce and some of its variations.

Basic White Sauce
(also known as Béchamel Sauce)
2 tablespoons butter
2 tablespoons flour
¼ teaspoon salt
1 to 1½ cups milk

Over medium-low heat, melt butter. Stir in flour and salt, whisking all the while to make what is known as a "roux". Cook and stir the roux-mixture for about 3 minutes (to cook-out the flour-pasty-flavor). Continuing to cook and stir, slowly add in the milk, whisking all the while until sauce is smooth and thickened. You now have your basic Béchamel Sauce, to which you can add many variations.

Variations:

Cheese Sauce
Lastly stir in ½ cup of shredded Cheddar cheese. Continue to stir and heat just until cheese melts.

Mornay Sauce
Lastly stir in ¼ cup grated Parmesan cheese, along with a pinch of nutmeg.

Sauce Moutarde
Lastly stir in 1 to 2 tablespoons Dijon-style mustard.

Veloute Sauce
Exchange the milk for chicken broth or chicken stock, and proceed as if making Béchamel sauce.

Secrets for Success:
Constant stirring with a whisk is elementary for making these smooth sauces.

Lightly season with salt and /or pepper to taste at very end of cooking time. White pepper is wonderful to use in these light-colored sauces.

Mom's Monday Hash

My mom used to make this meal the day after we had a roast. I have to admit I used to look forward to the hash more than the actual Sunday-roast dinner itself! She used to put the left-over meat and potatoes through a grinder—but who uses a grinder anymore! I just dice up my ingredients and go from there! As far as servings— this recipe really involves how much and many leftovers you have!

Leftover cooked beef, diced fine
Cooked potatoes, diced fine
Diced onion
Salt and pepper to taste
A pinch of garlic powder
A pinch of dried parsley flakes, crumbled between fingers
Evaporated milk (just enough to use as a moistener and binder)
Cooking oil, to cover bottom of pan
Ketchup, at serving time

Combine meat, potatoes, onion, seasonings and evaporated milk, mixing well. Brown hash mixture in medium-hot skillet (325 to 350 degrees) in enough hot cooking oil to cover bottom of pan. Cook until browned and crisped to your liking and all is heated through. Serve with a bottle of your favorite ketchup on the side.

Mom's secret ingredient was the evaporated milk used as a moistener and binder. She also used to 'put- up' her own ketchup—but I don't go that far either! (I can still see her standing over her pot of simmering tomatoes, ketchup splatters on her white apron and a scowl on her face at the mess she was making)—I think I'll just stick to bottled ketchup...

Hash a la Holstein

To Mom's Monday Hash add:
1 egg per person
Small pats of butter
Salt and pepper

When hash is almost done form "wells" in the hash, exposing bottom of pan. Put a little dab of butter in each well and carefully break an egg into each well. Salt and pepper the eggs. Cover and cook until eggs are set, but yolks are still soft. Serve each portion of hash to include a fried egg.

Secrets for Success:
Adding the eggs just takes this dish "over the top." (Why it's called "a la Holstein" I'll never know, because cows don't lay eggs...and chickens aren't Holsteins!)

June's 'Round-about' Chicken Hash

I am very lucky to have a wonderful neighbor who is also a wonderful cook. Her name is June and she has taken a "motherly" liking to me—I am even luckier because, many times when I get home from work, there is a "treat" waiting for me by my door...This recipe is one of those treats. One day I asked her how she made her hash...

Leftover cooked chicken meat, rustically diced (see chicken side note)
1 sweet onion, diced
Several red potatoes, peels left on, rustically diced
A pinch of salt
Sweet Hungarian Paprika (use a good quality paprika)
1 green bell pepper, ribbed and seeded, rustically cut
Canola oil, to cover bottom of skillet

Bring Canola oil up to temperature on a medium setting in skillet. Add onion, red potatoes, a little salt and sweet paprika. Cover and "slow-sauté" approximately 15 minutes, turning ingredients once or twice and always returning cover. Add chicken and season again with more paprika to arrive at a very orange color over all. Add green bell pepper and stir to mix all. Cover and cook for 5 to 6 minutes more, or until pepper pieces are tender but still slightly crisp. Total cooking time will be about 20 minute's tops. Do not over cook.

Secrets for Success:

The measuring of these ingredients (chicken, potatoes, onion and bell pepper) are totally up to you—to your taste and the amounts you have to work with. The secret ingredient for the dish however, is the liberal use of very good paprika (June visits a special spice store to get hers)—don't be shy when adding it. The success of the dish depends on orchestrating just the right amount of cooking time—the potatoes should be soft and the peppers still crisp, and the already-cooked chicken still moist and tender—every ingredient should have its own identity, yet be blended as well, into a sweet, paprika-y balance.

Chicken side note: June arrives at the leftover-cooked- chicken meat (for her hash) by first making a broth-style soup—A wonderful winter meal in itself, mind you— served with some crusty French bread and maybe a salad. She often makes a big pot of flavorful chicken soup—ending with a hearty but clear broth containing celery and carrots, and her special dumplings—but no chicken meat (or perhaps very little, depending on the mood she's in). All the flavor of the chicken has been artfully infused into her final delicate soup—leaving her with cooked chicken for her hash recipe! Sometimes, I find a container of her fabulous soup waiting for me first...then I know that in the next day or two, I will receive my second treat...the hash! – Isn't it nice to know that 2 such good recipes can be made from 1 chicken!

Mother's Potato and Egg Skillet

A classic for comfort—sometimes a breakfast meal at dinner time "fits the bill."

A large bag of frozen hash brown potatoes, thawed
Salt and pepper, to taste
1 tablespoon butter
Olive oil
1 egg per person, per serving
Additional butter
Beef-steak tomatoes, at serving time

On a medium to high heat setting, melt the butter into a little olive oil to cover bottom of pan. When oil is heated add hash browns to pan. Lightly season with salt and pepper to taste. Stir and sauté/fry until potatoes are nicely browned and thoroughly done. Make little "wells" in the potatoes, exposing bottom of pan. Put a dab of butter in each well. Carefully break an egg into each well. Cover and cook until eggs are fried to your liking and yolks are set but still soft. Do not over cook. Serve portions to include an egg in each serving. Serve with sliced beef-steak tomatoes to complete the meal.

Secrets for Success:

An initial pat of butter melted into the cooking oil gives the hash browns their flavor. Combining the butter in the oil keeps it from burning. Including an egg per person turns the recipe into a complete meal.

"Father Knows Best" Garden Ripe Beef-Steak Tomatoes

Want to see a kid eat a tomato?—serve it this way! (Adults like 'em too!)

Cut thick, juicy slices of vine-ripened tomato. Arrange on platter and sprinkle with sugar. Let stand till sugar dissolves into the tomatoes. Serve, room temperature, as a side dish, especially with potatoes and eggs.

Secrets for Success:

Adding a side dish of fresh tomatoes compliments any meal. Sprinkling them with sugar makes them very "kid friendly" and fun to eat. Never store your tomatoes in the refrigerator. Buy them fresh, store them on the kitchen counter where they can continue to ripen, and use them quickly—rather than storing in the fridge for days and days, only to have them loose both their flavor and their nutritional value.

Ham Slice Dinner

Salty verses sweet, sweet verses salty...

1 (3/4 to 1 –inch thick) fully-cooked ham slice
Non-stick cooking spray or a bit of fat trimmed from the ham
Serve with Sweet Surprise Rice (see recipe on next page)

To prepare ham for cooking trim off excess fat and cut slits around outside edge of ham slice. (This "scoring" will help prevent the edges from curling as you cook the ham.) Spray bottom of skillet with non-stick cooking spray, or rub pan with small piece of fat trimmed from the ham. On a medium heat setting brown ham slice in prepared pan about 3 to 5 minutes on each side, until lightly browned and heated through. Do not over cook. (Remember the ham is already cooked, so you just want to heat it.) Serve with Sweet Surprise Rice for a salt meets sweet combination.

Bonus Variation: For extra flavor you can spread Dijon-style mustard and brown sugar on the ham slice, just prior to cooking. When heated, this will melt to form a flavorful glaze on the meat. You can then elect to serve the ham with plain rice, or still use the Sweet Surprise Rice on the next page.

Sweet Surprise Rice

White or brown rice (use your favorite instant-style rice)
Packaged mixed-dried fruit (like a trail-mix variety that is all fruit,
  coconut and nuts, but no candy), or raisins and chopped nuts,
  or Craisins® (dried cranberries) and dried, chopped apricots
A dash of Sherry for flavor (optional)

Boil up rice according to package instructions.
Meanwhile chop dried-fruit mix into small, dice-sized
pieces. When rice is done, mix diced fruit of choice and a
dash of Sherry into the hot-cooked rice. Cover tightly,
remove from heat, and let fruit steam in rice for a few
minutes to soften. The fruit will soften yet remain a little
chewy. Serve as a contrasting side-dish with the salty
ham.

Secrets for Success:

The novelty of this dish is the contrast of the salty meat
with the fruit- sweetened rice. The amount and quality of
flavor in this dinner far exceeds its convenience and ease
of preparation—a complex medley of flavors, using
simple ingredients, to yield surprising results.

Mary and Bill's Macaroni and Cheese

There is life beyond Blue's Clues ™, *Rugrats* ™ *and boxed-macaroni mix! "Mac and Cheese" can be a dish for grown-ups too...*

1 pound elbow macaroni, cooked al dente, drained and set aside
3 tablespoons butter
2 tablespoons flour
2 cups whole milk
Salt and white pepper to taste
Dash of paprika (I like to use smoky, Spanish paprika)
2 cups shredded sharp Cheddar cheese
Sour cream, at serving time
Additional paprika, at serving time

On medium heat setting melt butter and then whisk in flour, making a roux for white sauce. Slowly whisk in whole milk and heat sauce, stirring all the while, until sauce becomes thickened and bubbly. Lightly season with salt, white pepper and a dash of paprika. Turn down heat setting to low and fold in Cheddar cheese. Continue stirring until cheese has melted and sauce is smooth and bubbly. Fold in cooked macaroni and toss until all is blended and coated well. Serve warm.

Secrets for Success:

Cook the macaroni just until al dente because you want it to hold up in the sauce. Use aged Cheddar cheese and whole milk to make a full-bodied sauce. For a variation try white Cheddar cheese. For extra richness garnish each serving with a dollop of sour cream and an extra sprinkle of paprika.

"Two Sandwiches for the Price of One"

Warm, pub-style sandwiches on a snowy night in Wisconsin—sounds good to me!

Recipe # 1

2 slices white bread per sandwich, crusts removed (optional)
Butter, softened for spreading
Sliced cooked chicken, preferably white breast meat, skin
  removed
A sprinkle of white pepper
A sprinkle of paprika
Roquefort, Gorgonzola or blue cheese, crumbled
Non-stick cooking spray
Jellied cranberry sauce, to serve as a garnish

Lightly and evenly butter bread slices (both sides) and trim off crusts (optional). Arrange sliced chicken meat on bottom piece of bread for each sandwich. Season lightly with white pepper and paprika. Cover with crumbled blue cheese of choice. Top sandwich with second slice of buttered bread and press down slightly. Heat skillet to 300 degrees and spray with non-stick cooking spray. Using your skillet as a griddle, grill the sandwiches till toasted and heated through, turning once. To serve, plate each sandwich and serve warm. Add a garnish of sliced jellied cranberry sauce placed on a lettuce leaf beside the sandwich.

Recipe # 2

Turn sandwiches into "Monte Christos." Assemble sandwiches as above, but omit buttering the bread and change the cheese to slices of Swiss. Dip assembled sandwiches in a beaten mixture of egg and milk—and proceed as if you were making French toast. Sauté egg-coated sandwiches until lightly browned on both sides, warmed through, and cheese is melt-y. Dust finished sandwiches with powdered sugar (for a true Monte Christo-style sandwich) and garnish with jellied cranberry slices.

Secrets for Success:

Both recipes, 1 and 2, are a great way to use up leftover chicken, or even turkey. For those who don't like blue cheeses try a crumbled goat cheese or Feta cheese. For kids, who like it mild, turn recipe # 1 into a "melt" by substituting American cheese or processed cheese slices, instead of blue cheese. Or, for a real treat, switch to Swiss cheese, dip your sandwiches in an egg wash and try recipe # 2.

MaryAnn's Italian Beef for Sandwiches

Half-cousin to the French Dip—this Italian sandwich makes a great, no-nonsense dinner...This recipe makes a lot and is great to freeze for "pull-out-of-the-freezer" meals on Monday nights or Sunday afternoons--while watching the "big game." Pile the meat high on good bread or buns, add some chips and condiments, and sit down to a real treat...

1 (3 to 4 pound) sirloin tip roast
1 teaspoon crushed oregano
2 teaspoons crushed basil
½ teaspoon crushed red pepper
½ teaspoon garlic powder
1 teaspoon celery salt
1 package dry onion soup mix
2 cups water
5 beef bouillon cubes

Mix dry ingredients (oregano through dry onion soup mix) together to form a "rub." Rub this mixture over surface of roast and pat into meat. Pre-heat your electric skillet on 350 –degree setting (while placing water and bouillon cubes in skillet). Place season-coated roast in center of the liquid filled skillet. Tightly cover and simmer roast for 30 minutes per pound at 350 degrees. If liquid evaporates too quickly turn down temperature setting, add additional liquid, and continue simmering until roast is succulent and tender. Remove roast from skillet and let rest 10 minutes before slicing. Slice thin.

Return meat slices to liquid in skillet and simmer to blend and coat. Serve warm on extra good buns or rolls. Toasting your rolls adds a nice touch.

Secrets for Success:

P.S. Obviously you don't have to be watching a football game to enjoy this recipe—as a good sandwich is popular almost anytime!

If you are having a party, try placing the meat filling on a horizontally-split whole loaf of French bread. Put top of loaf back on, and score at 1 1/2 –inch intervals. Brush top of loaf lightly with a bit of melted butter and sprinkle on a dusting of Parmesan cheese. (You can warm filled loaf slightly in a 300-degree oven if you wish, before serving.) Place in center of table as an "edible center piece. Let everyone cut off their portion-size from your 'giant sandwich' and garnish to taste with an assortment of condiments you have provided. Voila! Instant **Party Sandwich**!

Chapter Two:
That Special Touch

Filling and fancy entrees
with a special flair

This chapter is just what it says..."that special touch." Attention to detail, along with a bit of flair adds extra pizzazz to what could have been ordinary meals. Lemon-Orange Chicken to Swedish Meatballs, Swiss Steak to Turkey Stir Fry—all prepared with a special flair, a special spice or ingredient, and most of all—special care.

That Special Touch Index

Caleb's "Baked Chicken" Dinner for Two

Simple, straight forward—my son loved to make, and more importantly eat, this dish.

1 plump chicken, cut into halves, skin left on
2 tablespoons cooking oil
1 tablespoon butter
Paprika
Salt and Pepper
2 baking potatoes, pierced several times with a fork

Using kitchen shears or sharp Chef's knife, cut chicken into two neatly trimmed halves, removing any excess fat and excess skin. Set aside. Bring oil and butter up to temperature on 325 to 350-degree setting in skillet. Place chicken halves into skillet, skin side down, and brown until golden. Turn chicken over. Season with salt and pepper, and generously sprinkle with paprika. Place the baking potatoes along side chicken in skillet. Turn down temperature setting to 250 degrees and cover. "Bake" for approximately 1 hour, or until chicken is done (juices run clear) and potatoes are tender when pierced with a fork. (Turn potatoes half way through cooking time.) Invite your girl friend over for dinner.
--recipe printed in memory of Caleb Feiereisen, b. July 29th, 1970 d. October 4th, 1997

Secrets for Success:
Never underestimate simplicity.

Lemon-Orange Chicken

Lemons, oranges and wine make this truly a special dish. The addition of wild rice adds another sophisticated touch, but is not necessary. This recipe serves 6 (at 1 breast piece per person).

6 boneless, skinless chicken breasts
2 tablespoons Canola oil
1 tablespoon butter
6 garlic cloves, mashed and minced
½ cup shallots, minced
A pinch each: rosemary, parsley, paprika, salt and pepper
The juice from 2 oranges
The juice from 3 lemons
1 cup white wine, divided
*Cooked wild rice for serving (or substitute your favorite quick-cooking rice)

On medium to high heat setting (325 to 350 degrees) brown chicken breasts on both sides in heated cooking oil and butter. Add garlic, shallots and spices, and continue to sauté a few minutes more. Turn the heat down to simmer setting and pour on the orange and lemon juices, and ½ of the wine. Cover and simmer until chicken is cooked through and juices run clear (about 20-30 minutes). Remove chicken breasts and tent with foil on warm platter, or hold in 200-degree oven. Turn heat setting back up to 350-375 degrees and pour in the remaining wine. Cook uncovered until sauce reduces a bit. Add chicken back into skillet to mix with the sauce until glazed and heated through. Serve with cooked wild rice (or a wild rice blend, prepared according to package instructions).

Secrets for Success:

Reducing the sauce (at end of cooking) makes for full bodied, yet delicately flavored sauce. Using wild rice adds a nutty, robust contrast to the citrus-y sauce—yet this dish would be good with white or brown rice also.

*The Best Way to Prepare Wild Rice:

Living in wild-rice country, I've tried to prepare it many ways and this is my favorite for fluffy, fool-proof rice. Wild rice can be gummy and tough if not prepared correctly.

Boil a ratio of 1 cup wild rice per 4 cups water for 45 minutes, checking water from time to time so it doesn't foam over pot or scorch. After 40 to 45 minutes drain-off excess water and transfer rice to a towel-lined (the towel can be optional) colander. Place rice-filled colander over 1-inch of boiling water and cover pot with foil. Steam for at least 30 minutes till fluffy and tender. To serve, mix cooked rice with melted butter and sautéed mushrooms. Salt and pepper to taste. You can even add toasted nuts, raisins and a little sautéed onion if you wish. I like to make and freeze extra wild rice, re-steaming it as I need it, for quick dinners. Cooked wild rice keeps very well in the freezer.

Chicken "Vancouver" with Mushroom-Sherry Sauce

Sherry, Worcestershire and mushrooms take ho-hum chicken to a new level. Count on 1 chicken breast piece per person, for this tasty dish.

1 boneless, skinless chicken breast per person, rinsed and left wet
Pie plate of flour
Olive oil to cover bottom of pan
1 to 2 tablespoons butter
1 small onion, diced
Mashed and minced garlic cloves, to taste
1 small can of mushrooms, not drained
1 tablespoon Worcestershire sauce (or more to taste)
Water or chicken broth, as needed
2-3 tablespoons cooking Sherry (can be optional)
Salt and pepper to taste

Heat oil and butter on 350-degree setting. Add diced onion and mashed garlic cloves, and cook a few minutes to soften and flavor the oil. Push to the side of pan. Dredge wet chicken breasts in flour and gently brown on both sides in middle of pan (about 5 minutes per side). Stir in canned mushrooms (with their juice), Worcestershire, and a cup or so of water or broth. While stirring, loosen all the good browned bits in the pan and redistribute onions and garlic throughout. Turn down heat setting to simmer. Cover and simmer until chicken breasts are cooked through and juices run clear (about

20-30 minutes). Add more water or broth as necessary to keep pan moist and to make the amount of sauce that you desire. Toward end of cooking stir in cooking Sherry, and adjust seasonings with salt and pepper to taste. Serve with cooked rice, buttered noodles, or mashed potatoes.

Secrets for Success:

When dredging chicken, flour adheres better to wet chicken rather than dry. As the chicken cooks, you will find that the sauce will automatically thicken itself, from the initial dredging of the flour on the chicken, as some falls off into pan juices during cooking. Stir to combine this flour into the sauce.

A garlic tip: For convenience, I like to keep already mashed garlic on hand in the fridge. You can find prepared garlic, in little jars in the produce section of your favorite market. (I like to use the roasted variety.) That way you don't have to mess with sticky fingers and garlicky smell on your hands, as you prepare the garlic called for in your recipe.

The cooking Sherry can be optional to this recipe, but the Worcestershire is a must.

Gram's Chicken Marinara

This recipe is extremely flexible and really depends on what ingredients (and brands) you have in your well-stocked pantry. Count on 1 chicken breast piece per serving.

1 boneless, skinless chicken breast per person
2 to 3 tablespoons olive oil or any cooking oil
1 to 2 tablespoons butter or margarine
1 onion, finely chopped
1 tablespoon jarred, mashed garlic
Pre-made spaghetti sauce, your choice and to your liking
Water or chicken broth, your choice and to your liking
A dash of cooking Sherry or Madeira wine, for added depth and flavor
Just a tiny bit of sugar, white or brown
Shredded, low-fat cheese (your choice)
Cooked and buttered angel hair pasta (or pasta of your choice), for serving

Heat olive oil and butter to 325 degrees. Add finely chopped onion and prepared garlic to skillet and "caramelize" for about 5 minutes—until golden, but not burned. Push to edge of pan and add a bit more olive oil if necessary. Brown chicken breasts in center of skillet, about 5-7 minutes each side, turning once. Remove chicken from pan and set aside for just a minute. Stir in spaghetti sauce, water or broth, and a dash of cooking Sherry or Madeira wine. Stir to blend well, making a sauce to your liking. Add back chicken to skillet. Turn down heat setting, cover and simmer until chicken is cooked through and juices run clear (about 30 minutes).

Add more water as necessary, so sauce doesn't thicken too much and scorch. You can turn the chicken breasts over, as you are adjusting sauce to your liking. Cover and continue to cook. During last 5 minutes of cooking, place a generous portion of low-fat cheese on each chicken breast. Cover and continue cooking until cheese melts. While cheese is melting, cook up your (fast cooking) angel hair pasta in a pot of water that has been brought to a boil. (Angel hair only takes about 3 to 4 minutes to cook.) Drain and position pasta on individual plates. (You can toss pasta with a little butter if you wish.) Serve the chicken breasts on the individual beds of pasta, with the pan sauce drizzled over each serving. Let each person salt and pepper their own portion to taste.

Secrets for Success:

Make as little or as much sauce as you like. I find that sauces and gravies are a rather personal thing—so I leave the amounts of spaghetti sauce, water and/or broth, Sherry or Madeira, and sugar up to you. Customize this dish to the taste buds of your family Use as little or as much of the suggested ingredients as you like—or substitute whatever you have on hand in your pantry!

You can also use any style of pasta—I just happen to like angel hair because it cooks up so quickly. Angel hair pasta is a staple I always make sure to have stocked in my cupboard.

Chicken Piccatta-Style Sauté

Don't know what to make for dinner tonight?—Here is a quick and elegant way to prepare chicken breasts. Add a side dish or two and you have a simple but elegant meal.

Boneless, skinless chicken breasts (one per person)
Olive oil to cover bottom of pan
Water or chicken broth
1 package sliced fresh mushrooms
Cooking Sherry (optional for flavor)
A dash of Worcestershire, for flavor
Fresh lemon juice to taste
Jarred capers to taste

On a medium heat setting, gently brown chicken breasts in olive oil. Add a little water or chicken broth; turn temperature setting down a little; cover and simmer for about 25 to 30 minutes, or until chicken is cooked through, tender and juices run clear. Add more water during cooking process as/and if needed. Last 8 to 10 minutes of cooking add mushrooms, optional Sherry and a dash of Worcestershire. Last 5 minutes of cooking add the juice from a fresh lemon and capers to taste. Serve chicken drizzled with pan juices. Garnish with additional capers and a thin twist of lemon slice. Let people salt and pepper their dish to taste.

Secrets for Success:
Keep it simple. Keep it delicate. Keep it elegant.

"Menu Stretchers"

Suddenly you don't have enough for dinner! Someone brought an extra guest or a friend stopped by at the last minute. Or, maybe, you just didn't have quite as much ingredients as you had thought. That's where a well stocked pantry comes in handy. Prevent "dinner disaster" with a "menu stretcher" from your little treasure-trove of spontaneous necessities. (I know, I know—all through this book I have been advocating homemade! But once in a while even the best of cooks needs a little help adding to her dinner.) Here are some ideas to turn 'not enough' into 'plenty for all':

Jarred Applesauce or Canned Cranberry Sauce

Instant mashed potatoes (I'll never tell, if you won't)

Box-mix Blueberry Muffins or Corn Bread

A Side of Rice or Elbow Macaroni, when serving chili

Serve both a Vegetable and a Salad, or 2 vegetables instead of one

In a pinch extend a sauce with a can of soup or broth from your pantry

Serve a canned soup as a first course, in little cups with a garnish of croutons, and sour cream when applicable

Fresh fruit (when in season), garnishing each plate

A garnish of a slender green onion or crispy celery stalk on each plate, along with little "salts" for dipping.

After a lite dinner serve rich ice cream in pretty stemmed glasses, with a cookie or Twix® tucked on the side.

Chicken Stroganoff

We so often think of Beef Stroganoff, but chicken works equally as well. This recipe makes 4 rich servings.

4 to 5 boneless, skinless chicken breasts, to be cut into strips
2 tablespoons Canola oil
3 tablespoons butter
¼ cup finely minced shallots
½ teaspoon salt
¼ teaspoon white pepper
1 (10.5 ounce) can cream of mushroom soup
1 (3 ounce) can sliced mushrooms, including liquid
½ cup chicken broth
1 teaspoon bottled Maggi® seasoning
½ cup sour cream
Cooked noodles at serving time
Sprigs of chive for garnish

Heat oil and butter to 365 degrees. While oil is heating, cut each chicken breast into 10 or 12 strips. Quickly "stir fry" chicken strips in hot oil, for about 6 minutes. Add the shallots, salt and pepper, and cook 4 minutes more. Add the cream of mushroom soup, the mushrooms, with their liquid, and the chicken broth. Stir to combine. Turn down heat setting to 325 degrees. Continue cooking, stirring all the while until sauce just comes to a boil and is thickened and smooth. Stir in the Maggi® seasoning sauce. Turn down heat and at the last minute add the sour cream, stirring only to blend and heat through. Once the sour cream has been added do not let sauce boil. Serve over hot cooked noodles. Garnish each serving with freshly snipped sprigs of chive.

Secrets for Success:

This dish cooks up quickly, so have all your ingredients ready to go. Maggi® bottled seasoning may be found in the specialty-foods or condiment section of your market.

*As a side note: When cutting raw meats (especially chicken) into stir fry-size or thin strips, try putting the meat into the freezer for 10 minutes before slicing. This will firm up the meat, making slicing into thin strips neater and easier.

Beef Stroganoff

Although this dish requires a delicate touch and some practiced timing, the end result is well worth it. There is nothing better than a well executed, tender and rich, Beef Stroganoff and once you've made it a time or two you'll be a pro. This recipe serves 4 to 6 accompanied with cooked noodles.

1 pound sirloin beef steak, cut into ¼-inch thick, stir fry-size strips
2 tablespoons Canola oil
2 tablespoons butter
½ onion, diced
1 pound fresh mushrooms, sliced
1 teaspoon jarred, minced garlic
2 tablespoons additional butter
3 tablespoons flour
1 tablespoon lemon juice
1 tablespoon tomato paste
1¼ cups beef broth
1 cup sour cream
2 tablespoons Sherry or ½ cup white wine
1 teaspoon Kitchen Bouquet® or bottled Maggi® seasoning
Cooked noodles at serving time.

Heat Canola oil to 365 degrees. Quickly sauté the beef strips just till brown (but still rare and tender). Do not over cook. Remove from pan and set aside. Turn skillet down to 325 degrees. Add the first 2 tablespoons of butter, the onion, mushrooms and garlic. Sauté quickly for about 3-4 minutes. Add the second 2 tablespoons of butter and 3 tablespoons of flour to the skillet, stirring to make a roux (thick paste) cooking for 1 minute. Add the lemon juice, tomato paste and beef broth, cooking and stirring to make a smooth sauce. Add the beef strips back to the pan, heating just long enough to re-warm the meat. You do not want to over cook the meat (at the risk of it turning tough). Lastly stir in the sour cream, Sherry or wine, and the Kitchen Bouquet® or Maggi®. Cook only until heated through. Once the sour cream has been added do not let sauce boil. Serve immediately over cooked, buttered noodles.

Secrets for Success:

This is a dish that cooks up very quickly, so have all your ingredients ready to go and with-in arms' reach. Use a fine quality beef and do not over cook it. The biggest mistake with beef stroganoff is the over cooking of the ingredients—with the beef becoming tough and the sauce separating. Over-cooking the meat will take it from tender to tough. And over-heating the sour cream to a boiling point risks curdling and separation, making for an unsightly sauce.

Mrs. Shipley's "All American" Swiss Steak

All American?...or Swiss?...this dish (however it got its name) delivers homemade flavor for a tasty dinner for 6.

2 pounds round steak, cut 1-inch thick
1 cup flour for dredging
1 tablespoon dry mustard
1½ teaspoons salt
½ teaspoon black pepper
3 tablespoons Canola oil
1 large onion, sliced
2 cloves garlic, minced
2 large carrots, peeled and diced
4 cups coarsely chopped *peeled fresh tomatoes (or can use
  canned)
2 tablespoons Worcestershire sauce
1 tablespoon brown sugar
*Parsley buttered, boiled new potatoes, at serving time

Trim off any excess fat and cut meat into serving size pieces. Set aside. In pie plate, mix flour, dry mustard, salt and black pepper to season. Dredge steak pieces in seasoned flour, coating well. Press flour mixture into steaks to coat as well as you can. In electric skillet bring oil up to temperature at 350 to 365 degrees. Brown meat well on both sides. Sprinkle onion, garlic, carrots, Worcestershire and brown sugar over browned meat. Cover with the coarsely cut tomatoes. Cover pan and reduce heat setting to low-simmer. When tomatoes start to break up remove cover and stir to blend sauce. Turn meat pieces over in sauce. Replace cover and continue to gently simmer for about 1½ hours, or until meat is very tender, stirring once in a while to keep sauce from sticking. During cooking time add additional water as/and if necessary to keep sauce from reducing too much. Serve meat slices with pan juices drizzled over the top and parsley-buttered, boiled-red potatoes on the side.

Secrets for Success:

*To easily peel fresh tomatoes: Quickly plunge and lightly blanch in scalding water for about 30 seconds; then plunge into ice-water. Loosened skins will peel right off.

Parsley Buttered Boiled New Potatoes

In a pot of boiling, salted water to cover, cook new potatoes (mini-potatoes with tender red skins) "in their jackets" (peel left on) until fork tender (about 15-17 minutes, depending on size—if potatoes are large, cut them in half before cooking). Drain and drizzle with melted butter and sprinkle with fresh chopped parsley. Serve alongside Swiss steak. As a side note, parsley buttered boiled new potatoes make a nice accompaniment to almost any meal, and a nice diversion from every day mashed potatoes.

Sukiyaki Stir Fry
(10 ingredients, 10 minutes)

Here is a quick and delicious stir fry that takes only a few minutes of prep work and fewer minutes to cook. Have all your ingredients prepped in advance, because once you heat up the skillet cooking time only takes 10 minutes. This recipe makes 4 servings, and tastes wonderful and fresh and healthy.

Minute # 0) Using your electric skillet as if it were a wok, heat 3 tablespoons Canola oil to approximately 350 degrees—then continue as directed below:

Minute # 1) Add 1 large onion, sliced into rings and start "fast sautéing."

Minute # 2) Add a package of sliced, fresh mushrooms and continue sautéing.

Minute # 3) Add 1 pound of lean beef (such as flank or sirloin) that has been thinly sliced into stir fry-size strips and continue to fast sauté for no more than 2 minutes.

Minute # 5) Add ½ pound fresh spinach leaves (that have been cleaned, dried and de-veined).

Minute # 6) Add 3 (5-inch) stalks of celery that have been thinly sliced into julienne-style strips.

Minute # 7) Add 4 scallions (green onions) that have been cut into julienne-style strips (including tops).

Minute # 8) Add 4 tablespoons of soy sauce (regular or low-salt) and 2 tablespoons sugar.

Minute # 9) Add 1 can of beef broth and simmer just till heated through (no more than 2 minutes). Do not thicken sauce.

Serve immediately over your choice of cooked rice or cellophane noodles (very thin, transparent Oriental noodles that take about 2 minutes to re-constitute in hot water). Pass a garnish of crunchy chow mien noodles and additional soy sauce on the side.

Secrets for Success:

Placing the raw steak in the freezer for about 10 minutes will firm up the meat, making slicing into thin strips easier. Use a good cut of beef and cut strips across-the-grain. Cooking this dish for no more than 10 minutes keeps the meat tender and the vegetables crisp-tender. You do not want to over cook this dish.

Bonus Stir Fry Recipe

For a completely different variation replace the spinach with sliced bell pepper, or snow peas, or julienne-sliced green beans; omit sugar; cut the amount of soy sauce in half and add 2 tablespoons oyster sauce. Voila—a totally different stir fry in the same amount of minutes.

Secrets for Success:

You can find oyster sauce in the Oriental food section of your market.

June's Turkey Stir Fry

This delicious dish makes an awesome dinner for 8 lucky people.

2 packages JennieO Turkey Store® turkey breast tenderloin
   (about 2 pounds total), washed, patted dry on paper toweling
   and cut into generous bite-size pieces
1 large sweet onion, coarsely cut up
1 (8 ounce) package whole fresh mushrooms, cut into quarters
2 tablespoons Canola oil
1 tablespoon Dynasty® oyster sauce
1 teaspoon soy sauce
1 medium green bell pepper, cored, seeded and cut into strips
1 medium red bell pepper, cored, seeded and cut into strips
1 medium yellow bell pepper, cored, seeded and cut into strips
1 medium orange bell pepper, cored, seeded and cut into strips
Broccoli buds, cut from 1 generous stalk of broccoli
1 small zucchini, not peeled, cut into ½-inch thick slices
½ teaspoon additional soy sauce
1 tablespoon additional oyster sauce
Cooked white, brown or wild rice, for serving
Chow mien noodles, for garnish
Bottled soy sauce, to pass

Prep all meat and vegetables, cutting into sizes listed above, and set aside. On about a 350-degree setting bring 2 tablespoons Canola oil up to temperature. "Fast sauté" the turkey, onion and mushrooms in the heated oil. Quickly season with soy sauce and oyster sauce. Do not over cook. Remove mixture from skillet and set aside on warm platter (or in 200-degree oven) Add peppers, broccoli and zucchini to skillet. Season with the additional soy sauce and additional oyster sauce. Again quickly stir fry the vegetables in the hot skillet. You want the vegetables to be just getting tender, but still very crisp. Join the two mixtures by adding the reserved turkey mixture back to the skillet. Turn heat setting down and continue to cook about 7 minutes. (Turkey meat will cook very fast.) Again, do not overcook. You want everything to be done, but very crunchy, colorful and fresh. Serve immediately with hot white or brown rice (or wild rice). Pass crunchy chow mien noodles for garnish. Pass extra soy sauce to taste.

Secrets for Success:

There are two "musts" for this recipe—the ingredients of oyster sauce and turkey breast tenderloin; and secondly, having everything prepped and ready to go. Cooking it up quickly keeps the stir fry fresh and crunchy. June serves this dish with a simple side salad of fresh kiwi slices sprinkled with lemon juice.

Sea Scallops Moutarde with Fettuccini

Delicate and sublime, this rich seafood dish for 4 gets its subtle flavor from the combination of heavy cream, mustard and Sherry.

1 pound large scallops, each scallop sliced in half horizontally
4 tablespoons butter, divided
I cup sliced fresh mushrooms (or more to taste)
2 teaspoons Dijon-style mustard
A pinch of tarragon
12 ounces heavy cream (whipping cream)
¼ cup Sherry
Light seasonings of salt and white pepper
Linguini noodles, cooked "al dente" according to package
  directions
Grated Parmesan cheese

Over medium to high heat, bring 2 tablespoons of butter up to temperature. When butter is foaming sauté mushrooms about 5 minutes Add remaining 2 tablespoons of butter and the halved scallops. Sauté briefly, about another 5 minutes. Stir in mustard, tarragon and heavy cream. Lower heat setting and continue cooking (with out bringing to a boil) to thicken sauce for another 5 minutes. Flavor with the Sherry. Adjust seasonings to taste with salt and white pepper. Toss scallops and sauce over hot, cooked linguini noodles that have been reserved in a large pasta bowl. Garnish with grated Parmesan and serve immediately.

Secrets for Success:

Scallops are very delicate, very tender and cook-up quickly. Do not overcook at the risk of becoming tough, dried out and chewy.

Bonus Variation: a substitution of shrimp may be used to vary the dish. When doing so, add a little minced garlic while sautéing the mushrooms. (As with the scallops, do not over cook the shrimp.)

Sole au Beurre Amandine

The rich, nutty taste of browned butter with almonds, poured over a firm white fish perfectly sautéed (such as Sole, Flounder, Lake Trout or White fish) makes for a delectable fish dinner for family or company alike. For people who don't think they like fish, this is a dish to try... I might add for those anglers amongst us, North-woods walleye is an excellent candidate to receive this French interpretation... (Caleb used to catch 'em—I used to cook 'em...)

4 (4 -ounce) sole fillets, or other firm white fish
Flour for dredging, seasoned lightly with salt, white pepper and
  paprika
6 tablespoons butter, divided
Sliced, blanched almonds
Lemon wedges, at serving time

Dredge sole filets in seasoned flour to coat, shaking off any excess. On a medium-high heat setting, bring half of the butter up to foaming. Sauté fish filets no more than 3 to 4 minutes per side, or until opaque and flaky and gently cooked through. Remove to heated platter. Melt remaining butter in skillet until foamy. Add the almonds and sauté until golden brown. This needs a watchful eye, as almonds will cook quickly and get too dark. Pour the almonds and butter over the reserved fish. Serve immediately. Pass lemon wedges on the side.

Secrets for Success:
Do not overcook the fish. Do not over cook the almonds. Do not scorch the butter.

Linguine with Clam Sauce

This wonderful dish is so easy it is ridiculous! Amounts don't matter! Just keep adding until you arrive at what you need. This particular recipe serves 4 (at 1 can of clams per person), but can be adjusted any way you wish.

1 onion, chopped fine
Fresh garlic cloves, to taste, minced (I like to use a lot)
1/4 cup butter
3 cans clams, with their liquor (the juice in the can)
1 more can clams, drained
1 package shredded Monterey Jack cheese
Grated Parmesan cheese
White wine to taste (optional)
Salt and pepper to taste, and chives for garnish
Linguine pasta, cooked al dente
Freshly shaved Parmesan curls, at serving time

To make sauce, on a medium-high heat setting, melt butter. Add onion and garlic to skillet and gently sauté until softened. Add clams and juice, stirring to heat through. Add cheeses and keep stirring to melt and thicken sauce. Add a splash of white wine to taste and season lightly with salt and pepper. Keep stirring sauce all the while, so it doesn't stick to pan. (Sauce will be thin, thickened only by the cheese.) Season with salt and pepper to taste. Pour sauce over cooked linguini pasta and garnish with a sprinkling of minced chives (optional). Pass freshly grated Parmesan cheese curls on the side.

Secrets for Success:

Use a potato peeler to shave thin Parmesan curls from the side of a firm block of fine quality cheese. Nothing beats good, fresh Parmesan as a garnish!

Flank Steak Rollena

This braised, spicy, south of the border recipe will definitely tempt your taste buds. It's well worth the wait (let's face it, some recipes just can't be rushed). Prepare your stuffed flank steak on a lazy weekend afternoon and you'll have quite a meal.

1 large flank steak
1 clove garlic, peeled and smashed
½ pound Chorizo sausage, casing removed (or similar spicy sausage), broken up
2 green onions with tops, chopped
1 tablespoon chopped fresh parsley
1 tablespoon chopped green chili
1 egg
Flour for dredging steak
Canola oil to cover bottom of skillet
1 cup water
1 (15 ounce) can tomato sauce
½ cup beef broth
1 bay leaf

Rub both sides of flank steak with smashed garlic clove. Discard garlic clove. With a sharp knife "score" the flank steak on what will be the outside, making a diamond pattern of shallow cuts. Set aside. In a bowl, mix sausage meat, green onion, parsley, chili and the egg to make a stuffing. Lay the filling down the center of the un-scored side of the flank steak and roll up. Secure edges with toothpicks. Dredge the stuffed steak in flour. Brown on all sides in oil heated to 350 degrees. Add 1 cup water and lower heat to low- simmer setting. Cover and simmer for 1 hour. Add tomato sauce, broth and bay leaf.

Cover and continue to simmer until steak and filling are cooked through and steak is tender, about another ½ hour. Add more broth as/and if necessary, not letting pan dry out or scorch. When cooking is done, remove bay leaf from sauce. Remove toothpicks from flank steak and cut into serving-size slices. Serve with pan juices drizzled over steak slices. Add mashed potatoes and a refreshing fruit salad (see "Beyond the Pan" section for suggestions) to complete the meal.

Secrets for Success:

Flank steak is a very tasty cut of beef. It used to be very economical, but lately consumers have realized its culinary value and its price has risen dramatically—now making it a versatile and preferred cut of meat to be used in extended cooking.

A side note about flank steak in general: Flank steak works very well seasoned with marinades, quickly grilled or pan-seared to no more than medium rare—and then sliced very thin, cross-grain on the diagonal. Serve with baked potatoes and corn on the cob for a summer cook-out.

Betty's Braised Lamb with Burgundy

This is a succulent dish made with just a few ingredients. The depth of flavor comes from the long cooking time (using both browning and braising methods) along with the use of wine...Like I've said before some things are just well worth waiting for!

Lamb shoulder thick-cut (at least 1-inch thick) chops, 1 per
   person
Cooking oil, to cover bottom of pan
1 tablespoon butter
1 medium onion, cut into rings
1 cup water
4 to 5 carrots, peeled and broken into chunks
1 cup Burgundy table wine
Canned beef bouillon
1 to 2 tablespoons flour, mixed into a little water in a screw top
   jar
Salt and pepper to taste
1 additional tablespoon butter
Hot buttered broad noodles at time of serving

Set your skillet at about 325 to 350 degrees and bring cooking oil and butter up to temperature. Brown shoulder chops for about 20 minutes (10 minutes per side). Add onion rings and sauté slightly. Add water. Add carrots and Burgundy. Turn heat setting down to low-simmer, cover tightly and "braise" (i.e. very slow, covered simmering, after initial browning, to yield tender meat) for 1½ to maybe 2 hours (time will depend on thickness of meat). Last ½ hour of cooking add 1 cup canned beef bouillon, cover and continue cooking. When chops are very tender, remove to warm platter and hold in 250 oven (while making gravy from the pan juices). To make gravy, skim off any excess surface fat from pan juices. Turn skillet setting back up to 350 degrees. Stir in the flour/water mixture, cooking and stirring all the while to thicken pan juices. Add extra bouillon as needed, to arrive at amount and consistency of gravy you desire. At the last minute swirl in 1 tablespoon of butter to "finish" the sauce. Adjust seasoning with salt and pepper. Serve chops with hot buttered broad noodles, pan gravy, and a side vegetable of Sugared Peas (see my secret for success page 21).

Secrets for Success:

For the bouillon you can use either ready-made canned— or cubes or crystals dissolved in water according to package instructions. You might try varying this recipe with chicken bouillon and white wine for a lighter flavor. You can also cut slits into the chops and insert pieces of garlic clove directly into the meat (before browning) to "infuse" additional flavor if you wish. Also, as in any of the dishes offered in this cookbook, that ask for wine— you may alter the recipe to your taste by substituting beef, chicken, or vegetable broth, or water in place of the wine. Cooking is an art and everyone's "palette and palate" are different! Half the fun of cooking is taking a suggested recipe and using it as a guideline to create your own recipe to your own personal preferences— adding and deleting items as you wish.

Caleb's Beef with Onions and Beer

A true bachelor's dish—filling and easy—and of course it includes beer. This recipe makes 4 servings, when the guys come over.

1½ pounds (¾ -inch thick) round steak, cut into serving size
   pieces
Pie plate of flour for dredging
1 stick butter, divided in half
1 very large onion, sliced
1 teaspoon Dijon mustard
A dash of Worcestershire
1 bottle of beer
4 peeled garlic cloves
Salt and pepper to taste

Cut round steak into serving size pieces and dredge in flour. Set aside. Meanwhile set skillet setting to 325 degrees and heat ½ stick butter till melted. Add onions to skillet and sauté until onions are soft and golden. Remove onions from skillet and set aside. Add second portion of butter to melt. Now brown the floured meat on both sides. When meat has browned add back onions, stir in mustard and a dash of Worcestershire. Pour on the bottle of beer and add the 4 garlic cloves. Season with a little salt and pepper. When beer starts to boil, turn down heat setting to low-simmer and cover. Simmer for 1 to 1½ hours, or until meat is very tender. Add more beer or water as/and if necessary during the cooking process. Remove the 4 garlic cloves before serving. While dinner is cooking bake up some potatoes and steam some broccoli.

Secrets for Success:

This dinner is both economical and filling, and includes simple ingredients most guys (like my son) would readily have on hand. Cooking the onions to a "caramelized" state and then browning the meat in the resultant-onion-flavored oil is an easy way to add depth and flavor to the dish. (I dare say my son didn't realize what a good cook he was!)

Savory Pot Roast Koopmann

With hints of sweet and sour, and old fashioned-Sauerbraten flavors, this is a favorite in the Koopmann's mid-western household.

1 (3 ½ to 4 pound) chuck roast
2 large onions, coarsely cut
1 tablespoon brown sugar
1 teaspoon salt
3 tablespoons catsup
2 tablespoons cider vinegar
2 bay leaves
16 ounces of 7-UP®
½ cup raisins

Place chuck roast in skillet. Add remaining ingredients. Cover and bring up to boil. Lower temperature and simmer until tender. Turn roast from time to time during this extended cooking process. (Count on about 45 minutes per pound on a setting of 225 degrees.) Remove bay leaves at end of cooking. Serve sliced, with mashed potatoes (or dumplings) and your favorite side dishes.

Secrets for Success:

Brown sugar and cider vinegar are musts for this recipe. For another flavor try adding Dr. Pepper® in place of 7-UP®. Spaetzle or dumplings add yet more European flare.

Portuguese Pot Roast

My friend Fay makes the best pot roast imaginable...her secret...sweet, rich, Port wine!

1 (2 to 3 pound) boneless pot roast
2 tablespoons cooking oil
½ cup water
Salt and pepper to taste
1 large onion, peeled and chopped
4 to 6 carrots, scrubbed and cut in half
2 stalks of celery, de-ribbed and cut in thirds
2 large potatoes, scrubbed and cut in quarters
½ cup Port, or similar heavy, sweet wine
An additional splash of Port, when making gravy

Bring oil up to temperature on a 360-degree heat setting. Quickly brown pot roast on all sides in hot oil. Season with salt and pepper and add ½ cup water. Turn down heat setting to simmer and cook covered, until meat is very tender (about 2 hours). Add more water, as and if necessary during extended cooking process. Last hour of cooking add the onion, carrots, celery and potatoes and pour in the Port. When meat and vegetables are done, remove to platter and thicken skillet-juices to make gravy of desired consistency. Flavor gravy with an additional splash of Port while thickening. Check and adjust seasonings with more salt and pepper, if needed. Serve pot roast sliced, passing gravy on the side. Add mashed potatoes or noodles to complete the meal.

Secrets for Success:
—Long, lazy, slow cooking and a generous splash of Port.

MaryAnn's 1-2-3-4-5 Country-style Ribs

A five-ingredient sauce and a batch of country-style ribs make this dish a delectable treat.

1 to 2 pounds country-style beef ribs, each rib cut into thirds
1 tablespoon Sherry
2 tablespoons dark soy sauce
3 tablespoons apple cider
4 tablespoons sugar
5 tablespoons water

Combine ingredients 2 through 6 in a covered electric skillet. Heat until sugar dissolves and liquid is simmering. Add rib-pieces to skillet. Cover and cook at 325 to 350 degrees for 40 minutes. Do not open lid! After 40 minutes, remove cover, turn ribs and continue to cook just to caramelize the liquid, being very careful not to scorch sauce. Turn off heat setting immediately when done and serve; or remove ribs with their glaze to a warm platter and serve.

Secrets for Success:

1-2-3-4-5—you don't have to be a mathematician to enjoy this dish!

MaryAnn's Mushroom Meatballs

MaryAnn Koopmann is a cook after my own heart...a realistic cook, serving real food from her country-style kitchen—I am very fortunate to have her added recipes to this book.

1 pound lean ground beef
1 can mushroom soup, divided
½ cup breadcrumbs
2 tablespoons minced onion
1 tablespoon minced parsley
1 egg, beaten
1 to 2 tablespoons shortening
½ cup water

Into a mixing bowl, divide out ¼ cup of the mushroom soup and reserve the rest. Lightly mix ground beef with the ¼ cup soup, breadcrumbs, onion, parsley and egg to make meatball mixture. Do not over-work mixture. Gently shape into "golf ball"-sized balls. Melt the shortening in skillet set at 350 degrees. Brown meatballs on all sides. When nicely browned, combine remaining soup with water and pour over meatballs. Turn down heat setting, cover and simmer for 15 minutes. Serve over noodles or mashed potatoes.

Secrets for Success:

Remember to lightly mix and gently form your meatball mixture. Spray a little non-stick cooking spray on your hands so mixture doesn't stick.

Harriet's Family-Favorite Veal Meatballs

Slowly simmered in their own gravy, with hints of sage and nutmeg, Harriet's veal meatballs have been dubbed a family favorite by her sons and grandsons—truly a man's meal.

1 pound ground veal
¼ pound ground pork
1 egg
¼ cup finely chopped onion
1 cup crumbled saltines
1 teaspoon salt
½ teaspoon sage
¾ teaspoon nutmeg
Pie plate of flour for dredging
2 tablespoons Canola oil
2 tablespoons butter
Canned chicken broth

In a large bowl lightly mix together first 8 ingredients until blended. Do not over mix or over work, or the meat balls will become tough. With your hands, lightly form and roll the meat/mixture into fist-sized balls. Dredge the meatballs in flour. Set the skillet on 350-degree setting, and bring oil and butter up to temperature. Brown the meat balls on all sides, adding more butter if/and as needed. Add canned chicken broth, cover, and reduce setting to low-simmer. Simmer meatballs, in their own gravy, for 1 hour. (At end of cooking time you can make additional gravy if needed, by adding 1 tablespoon of flour/mixed with a little broth to the skillet. Then add additional broth, stirring and cooking, to arrive at the amount and consistency of "pan gravy" you desire.) Serve with mashed potatoes or hot buttered noodles and a nice side salad (see Beyond the Pan Section).

Secrets for Success:

The keys to this dish are the combination of seasonings and the slow simmering. Also, when "building" your meatballs do not over work your meat mixture—you want your meatballs to be light and tender, before they even get to the pan.

Mrs. Larson's Swedish Meatballs

When I was a little girl my parents used to travel quite frequently on extended business trips, so they hired a wonderful Swedish woman, named Mrs. Larson, to take care of me. I used to love when she came to stay at my house. Eventually I grew up and she returned to Sweden. One day I wrote to her, asking for my two favorite recipes. Her letter came back in rather broken English and elderly handwriting, but I was thrilled to have retrieved her wonderful recipes!

1 to 1½ pounds ground beef
1/3 cup dry bread crumbs
½ cup finely chopped onion
½ teaspoon salt
¼ teaspoon pepper
¼ teaspoon allspice
2/3 cup canned evaporated milk
3 tablespoons butter, and more if needed
2 bouillon cubes (or the equivalent in crystals) dissolved in 1
   cup hot water
¼ cup flour/mixed with a little water to form a thickening agent
¼ teaspoon additional allspice
½ cup water
1 cup canned evaporated milk
1 tablespoon lemon juice
Hot buttered noodles at serving time

In a bowl lightly mix first 7 ingredients together. Do not over work. Form meat mixture into approximately golf ball-size meatballs. While forming meatballs set skillet on 325-degree setting and melt in 3 tablespoons of butter. Gently brown meatballs (in batches if need be) in butter, adding more butter per batch if necessary. As you brown the meatballs (if you are working in batches) remove them to a warm platter and hold in warm oven. When you are done browning, add dissolved bouillon to the skillet. Reduce heat setting to simmer, add all meatballs back to pan, cover and simmer for 10 to 15 minutes. Uncover and slowly add flour/mixture and then ½ cup water to pan, stirring all the while to start making gravy. As sauce cooks and thickens stir in the evaporated milk and the additional allspice. Continue cooking and stirring until all is heated through, thickened and smooth. Lastly stir in the lemon juice. Serve immediately with hot buttered noodles.

Secrets for Success:

Don't be afraid to try something old fashioned and make it new for your family. If you wish, sour cream may be substituted in place of the last portion of evaporated milk. If so, eliminate the lemon juice, add the sour cream and do not let sauce come to a boil.

Pineapple Pork Chops

Sweet, yet tangy, the combination of pineapple and onion offers an intriguing flair to your pork chop menu. Count on 1 pork chop per person. Add a special garnish to the plate and you have a dinner decorated for company.

4 to 6 lean loin cut pork chops, 1-inch thick, well trimmed of fat
1 to 2 tablespoons Canola oil
Salt and pepper to taste
1 (1 pound can) pineapple chunks, juice packed, drained with
  juice reserved
½ cup plum jam
1 tablespoon vinegar
1 tablespoon soy sauce
1 teaspoon Worcestershire sauce
½ teaspoon jarred, prepared ginger (or grated fresh ginger root)
4 scallions, with tops, sliced julienne style
Hot cooked, instant rice (white or brown) at serving time
*Extra green onions (scallions) for garnish at serving time

In electric skillet bring a little Canola oil up to temperature (350 degrees). Brown pork chops well on both sides. Lightly salt and pepper chops. While chops are browning, in a bowl combine ½ cup reserved pineapple juice with plum jam, vinegar, soy sauce, Worcestershire and ginger to make a sauce. Reduce heat setting to simmer and pour sauce over chops. Cover and slowly cook chops for 25 to 30 minutes, adding any remaining pineapple juice as/and if necessary. Lastly fold in pineapple chunks and julienne-sliced onions, cooking until all is heated through. Plate chops, drizzled with sauce. Add hot cooked rice on the side. Garnish each plate with a crisp green onion frill.

Secrets for Success:

As on option to fresh ginger root, you can find prepared-jarred ginger in the same produce section of your market—usually located right next to the conveniently-jarred garlic. Store in refrigerator to keep handy anytime a recipe calls for ginger.

*To make Fancy Green Onion Frills—begin by neatly trimming both ends of onion. With a sharp paring knife, cut several thin, ribbon-like slits thru one or both ends of the onion, drawing the knife from the middle out to the end as you carefully make each cut. When finished cutting plunge (and store) prepared onions in ice water until ready to use. The cold water will cause the cuts to curl and "ribbon"—making for a fancy garnish. Drain and use as an edible decoration on each plate.

*Celery stalks can be thinly ribbon-ed and flared using the same method.

*Radish Roses can be made using the same method also. Trim top and bottom off radish. Make several rounds of thin, petal-shaped cuts around the top and down the sides of the radish, slicing your "petals" as thin as possible. Plunge and store in ice-water. The radish will "open" and "flower" into a beautiful garnish, making a colorful addition to any plate. Drain off excess water when serving.

Mrs. Larson's Swedish Pancakes

I know... I know... This isn't exactly a dinner recipe, but when I was little I used to beg my Swedish baby sitter, Mrs. Larson, to make these. If I was reeeeally good she would let me have her Swedish pancakes for dinner! To this day I regard these as one of my utmost comfort foods—so the next time you want breakfast for dinner...or need a little batch of tender lovin' care, try these delicious pancakes! This recipe makes 4 servings—although I must admit I could eat the whole thing!

3 eggs
1 tablespoon sugar
½ teaspoon salt
1 cup flour
2 cups whole milk
Butter for cooking
Applesauce for serving

Beat first 5 ingredients to form a very smooth batter. Using your skillet as a griddle, heat butter in bottom of pan till hot and sizzling-bubbly, but not burning. Spoon batter into hot skillet and spread with spoon to form about an 8-inch circular pancake. Cook until gently browned, then carefully flip each tender pancake and brown second side. As you cook them, remove and stack on a warm plate and hold in a warm oven. Top each pancake with a bit of butter as you place it on the stack. When you have finished your stack of pancakes, spread applesauce over the top. Serve immediately, cutting into 4 wedges, as if you were cutting a cake. Additional applesauce may be served on the side, along with a dusting of cinnamon if you wish.

Secrets for Success:

The trick to cooking these tender pancakes is the temperature of the butter—hot and sizzling and foamy but not burning, so you get just the right golden brown, lacy pattern on each side of each pancake. The stack of pancakes should be tender and spongy, warm and buttery-rich—just waiting for the topping of contrasting applesauce.

Bush's ®
"CaribBean" One Pot Stew

A blending of ginger, cumin, sweet potatoes and Bush's Best® beans, along with seasoned pork, makes for an exotic mix of flavors to please any dining table. This recipe is written to make 3 quarts and serves 8 guests, but could easily be cut in half.

1 pound sweet potatoes (about 2 medium potatoes), *cooked,
   cooled, peeled and cut into ½-inch cubes
2 tablespoons olive oil
2 tablespoons minced ginger
3 garlic cloves, minced
¼ jalapeno, minced
2 stalks celery, diced
1 green bell pepper, diced
1 small onion, diced
1 pound pork loin, trimmed and cut into ½-inch pieces
1 teaspoon ground cumin
½ teaspoon salt
¼ teaspoon ground black pepper
3 (16 ounce) cans Bush's Best® dark red kidney beans, rinsed
   and drained
1 (14.5 ounce) diced tomatoes
1 (14.5 ounce) can chicken broth
Bottled hot sauce, at serving time

With a setting of about 325 to 350 degrees, bring 2 tablespoons olive oil up to temperature. Gently sauté ginger, garlic and jalapeno until soft (about 2 minutes). Add celery, green pepper and onion, and cook until translucent (about 5 minutes). Season pork pieces with cumin, salt and pepper. Add to skillet and sauté to brown on all sides. Add Bush's Best® dark red kidney beans, tomatoes, broth and sweet potato-pieces. Bring just to boiling, then reduce temperature setting to simmer. Simmer mixture for 25 to 30 minutes, or until pork is tender. Adjust seasonings to taste and serve. Pass hot sauce on the side if desired.

--recipe courtesy of Chef Katy Keck on behalf of Bush's Best® Beans

Secrets for Success:

—A Tip from the Kitchen of Bush's Best® Beans: "When prepping sweet potatoes for use in this recipe, prick sweet potatoes with a fork and microwave on high for 6 to 8 minutes until tender. Set aside. When cool peel and cut into ½-inch cubes for use in the recipe."

Beef Sandwiches a la Stroganoff

"Open-faced" sandwiches turn every day leftovers into a fancy meal. My mom used to make these as a way of using up leftover roast beef.

1 tablespoon butter
1 tablespoon minced onion or shallot
1 small can mushroom slices or pieces, drained
1 (10.5 ounce) can (or jarred) mushroom gravy
1 tablespoon cooking Sherry or 1 teaspoon Worcestershire sauce
½ cup sour cream, or to taste
Sliced leftover roast beef
Buttered slices of toast or toast points for "open faced" sandwiches
Snips of freshly picked chive for garnish (optional)

On 325 to 350-degree setting melt butter into skillet. Sauté onion until tender and softened. Add mushrooms and sauté 1 minute. Add canned or jarred gravy and the Sherry or Worcestershire sauce, stirring to make smooth sauce. Stir in slices of leftover roast beef. Lower heat setting and stir in sour cream. Cook until all is heated through, about 5 minutes in all. Do not bring sauce to a boil once sour cream has been added. Arrange meat slices with sauce, on buttered toast or buttered "toast points." Serve "open faced" garnished with snips of chive. Accompany with a salad from the Beyond the Pan section to complete the meal.

Secrets for Success:

This is a great way to utilize leftover roast beef (or steak) from a previous dinner—or buy deli roast beef if you don't have leftover meat. Be sure to butter the toast for extra-rich flavor! For an alternate version try leftover chicken in place of the beef.

"Beyond the Parsley"— Optional Garnishes

Fun and fancy, garnishes add that special detail to make any meal memorable—a little bonus—a delightful "Lagniappe" if you will—making your presentation artful and "signatured"—raising the dish from humble to an offering with flair.

The garnish can be as simple as toasted nuts or as elaborate as a long tomato peel, curled up to make a rose. Celery sticks, scallions, and radishes are ready made candidates for carving into graceful ribbon-ed shapes (see page 130).

A little cluster of mini-champagne grapes, or a fanned-out strawberry, or a slice of seasonal fruit might be just what you want. The fruit can even be frosted with a dusting of sugar.

A sprinkling of lemon, lime or orange-peel curls, (made with a potato peeler or zesting tool, (or a thinly sliced twist of the appropriate citrus fruit) can compliment what has already been cooked in the dish.

Stalks of freshly snipped chive can offer an architectural and visual touch, casually arranged at the last minute.

If you've used paprika, try a final sprinkle for extra color.

Thinly sliced Parmesan cheese curls can be made with a potato peeler, and offer a nice variation from the every day use of grated Parmesan.

—Or how about a pansy or nasturtium blossom—tucked directly from your garden onto the plate.

Secrets for Success:

The options are endless. Be creative. Be fun. Make your plate a personal "palette"—feed your eye as well as your tummy. If nothing else, an intriguing and unexpected garnish can be a great starter for dinner conversation!— and what better "garnish" can you have for a meal...good company, vibrant conversation and plenty of compliments!

Chapter Three:
Simply Sensational
Specialty dishes for creative cooking

Simply Sensational is a chapter that will get you rave reviews. From Chicken Kiev to Chipotle Sauce, from Beef Medallions to Steak Diane, the creative cook takes center stage in this kitchen. Complete instructions take the difficulty out of these gourmet offerings, as you move step by step into more adventuresome cooking.

Simply Sensational Index

Chicken Kiev

This is one of my favorite chicken dishes. Slightly labor intensive—but follow a few special rules and you will have a classic meal fit for royalty. This recipe is written to make 8 homemade-buttery Kievs.

4 large, boneless, skinless chicken breasts, halved into 8 cutlets, each pounded thin
Plastic wrap or waxed paper, and a mallet or wooden spoon
Salt and pepper to taste
1 (¼ -pound) stick icy cold butter, to be divided into 8 slices
2 to 3 tablespoons snipped fresh chives, to be divided
1 green onion, finely diced to include top, to be divided
2 tablespoons grated Parmesan cheese (optional), to be divided
Water
Flour in a pie plate
1 egg, beaten with 1 tablespoon water
Dry bread crumbs in a pie plate (plain or seasoned, your choice)
Tooth picks
Canola oil to generously cover bottom of skillet to depth of ¼ -inch

Rinse chicken breasts with cold water and pat dry with paper toweling. Carefully slice each chicken breast horizontally into 2 thin cutlets. Sandwiching each cutlet between layers of plastic wrap or waxed paper, pound with a mallet, rolling pin (or the back of a sturdy wooden spoon) to ¼ –inch thickness. Remove wrap and lightly season what is going to be the interior side with salt and pepper. For filling, cut stick of cold butter in half, and then divide each half into 4 (half-stick-length) slices, ending with 8 elongated pieces of cold butter that equal about 1 tablespoon each. Place 1 cold slice of butter on each cutlet. Sprinkle chives, green onion and grated Parmesan cheese over butter. Roll up "jelly-roll fashion" tucking in sides and ends—so seasoned butter is totally contained in the center of each rolled cutlet. Secure final edge with a toothpick if necessary. Moisten chicken with water. Roll wet chicken in flour to coat well; then in beaten egg mixture to coat well; then in breadcrumbs to coat well and evenly. For best results, return prepped chicken rolls (covered again with plastic wrap) back to refrigerator for about an hour before cooking. (You can make these ahead and hold in refrigerator until cooking time.) Bring Canola oil up to a temperature of 365 degrees. Using tongs, carefully place chilled chicken rolls into the hot oil. Quick-sauté until golden brown, on both sides, and meat is cooked through (all the while keeping the chilled butter and seasonings contained inside). The chicken will cook quickly and should take no more than 5 to 6 minutes per side. If you feel the chicken is browning too quickly, turn heat setting down to continue cooking just until done. Be careful not to overcook as butter filling will melt and start to run out the sides. (Remember, you are trying to keep the butter contained inside.) With tongs remove chicken rolls from skillet and drain on paper toweling while removing any toothpicks. Serve immediately, accompanied with a nice salad and crusty French bread.

Secrets for Success:

Pounding the chicken thin, using chilled ingredients, and quick-sautéing (refer to 'shallow-pan, deep-frying method on page 17), helps to successfully contain the classic butter-filling inside the rolled chicken. The goal is to have the butter spill out as you cut into your serving. Some recipes call for additions of minced garlic and/or minced parsley, but I personally prefer featuring just the chives, green onion and Parmesan.

Chives: Chives are one of the easiest of herbs to grow on a sunny windowsill, in a pot on a patio or balcony, or in an herb garden. They are one of the first to pop up in the spring and they are hardy and durable until late fall. I love to go outside and pick fresh chives to garnish my dinners and salads. Late in the season harvest remaining chives, chop and freeze in an air-tight baggy for winter use.

Chicken-Safety: When working with raw chicken (and this goes for any recipe and raw meat) always wash your hands and any kitchen surfaces, cutting boards, plates, utensils, etc. that have come in contact with the raw chicken (or meat). Discard any excess bread crumbs, egg wash, raw marinades, etc. that are leftover from dredging, dipping, seasoning, etc. after their use. After removing chicken from store-bought package, wash with cold water and pat dry on paper toweling before proceeding with recipe.—Raw chicken should be used within 2 days of purchase. Always choose chicken that looks plump, fresh and has no smell. Avoid packages that have runny juices or pinkish-crystals (indicating freezing-thawing-refreezing) and always check sale date on package. Frozen chicken packages should always be thawed in the refrigerator, or in water-tight, sealed wrapping plunged into cold water—never just on the counter at room temperature.

Betty's Chicken Royale

Once in a while mother would make this special dish and I have mouth-wateringly carried on the recipe. The combination of chicken, stuffing and rich sauce are truly "royale" to say the least—a great dish to serve for a fancy dinner for 4.

4 plump chicken breasts, boned and butter-flied, or cut to have
   a pocket in each to hold bread stuffing. Wash and pat dry.
1 cup flour
½ teaspoon salt
½ teaspoon paprika
¼ teaspoon ground black pepper
A paper grocery bag
2 cups of good quality bread stuffing (My mother used
   Pepperidge Farms®)
Tooth picks
Cooking oil and 1 tablespoon butter for frying
1 stick butter, melted
1 package sliced fresh mushrooms
¼ cup diced onion
2 tablespoons additional butter
2 tablespoons flour
½ cup cream (I use half-and-half cream)
½ cup sour cream
½ teaspoon additional salt
¼ teaspoon additional pepper

Place flour, salt, paprika and pepper in a paper grocery bag and mix well. Put chicken in paper bag and shake to coat well. Fill each chicken breast (to bulging) with bread stuffing. Secure openings with toothpicks to hold in stuffing. Bring cooking oil and butter up to medium-high temperature in skillet and quickly brown breasts on both sides until golden. Turn down heat setting. Drizzle on melted butter, cover and gently cook chicken about 40 minutes, or until juices run clear (turning once). Cooking time will depend on thickness of chicken and amount of stuffing used. When chicken is done, temporarily remove and hold in 200-degree oven. To the skillet juices add the mushrooms and sauté for several minutes. Stir in the additional 2 tablespoons of butter and the flour to make a roux for thickening the sauce. Add cream, sour cream and adjust salt and pepper to taste, stirring to thicken to a rich sauce. Do not boil. Return chicken breasts to skillet until all is heated through. Serve chicken with skillet sauce spooned over all. Accompany with a simple, steamed side vegetable such as broccoli, and blueberry or cornbread muffins (conveniently made from a boxed mix or picked up at your favorite bakery).

Secrets for Success:

The use of butter and cream are key to this admittedly sinful dish—but for a splurge this dish is well justified. Serve with a simple steamed vegetable to cleanse the palate and off-set the richness of the meal.

Chicken "Cordon Blue"

This is a favorite of my daughter's. My cookbook wouldn't be complete without a recipe for this complex, yet easy to prepare dish. Your electric skillet is a natural in which to prepare this salty, cheesy, melt-y, succulent version. Base your recipe on 1 Cordon Blue per person.

1 chicken breast per person, washed and patted dry
1 slice of deli ham for each portion (or cooked Canadian bacon or leftover ham)
1 slice Swiss cheese for each portion (or string cheese sticks work as well)
A little diced onion
Minced garlic to taste (can use jarred)
Olive oil, for sautéing onion/garlic, and then the chicken
Water, for moistening chicken (optional)
Flour, for coating chicken (optional)
Additional olive oil, for browning chicken rolls
A little water or chicken broth, for simmering
Freshly cracked pepper
Whole cooked shrimp, for garnish (optional)

Gently sauté diced onion and garlic in a little olive oil on medium heat setting to soften and turn golden, being careful not to burn garlic! Remove onion/garlic mixture from skillet and set aside, retaining flavored oil in skillet. Carefully slice chicken breasts horizontally through the middle and open up like a "butterfly." Smear each opened chicken breast with the cooked onion/garlic mixture and season with freshly ground pepper. For filling, roll a ham slice around a cheese slice. Place in center of chicken and fold up, envelope-style, to contain filling. Secure with toothpicks, if needed, to hold filling inside. Moisten surface of assembled chicken with water. Dredge wet chicken in flour, coating well. (This process can be omitted if you wish, just using filled chicken as is.) Add more olive oil to the already flavored oil in skillet and "bring up to temperature".   Sauté filled breasts (flour-coated or not, your choice) browning both sides until golden. Add a little water or broth to skillet. Cover and simmer for 20 to 30 minutes, or only until chicken is done and all is heated through. (Cooking time will very with size and thickness of filled breasts.) Add more water or broth as/and if necessary to prevent everything from sticking to pan. (Sometimes the cheese has a tendency to melt out of the center and start to thicken and stick.) When done remove Cordon Blues to individual plates. If you wish, drizzle tops of each with any pan juices remaining. Garnish each serving with a cooked shrimp (optional) perched on top. Serve with a simple vegetable and blueberry muffins.

Secrets for Success:

No salt or pepper is needed for this dish. The ham, cheese, and lightly sautéed onion/garlic provide the entire flavors needed. The shrimp garnish adds extra flair.

Coq au Vin

Rich and warming, this farmhouse-French recipe is written to serve 6.

4 slices bacon, diced
1 whole chicken, cut into pieces, and 2 extra breast pieces
12 pearl onions
12 whole button mushrooms
2 cloves garlic, mashed and minced
About 6 green onions (including tops), cut up
¼ cup flour
2 cups good red table wine
2 cups chicken broth
1 teaspoon salt
Freshly cracked pepper
½ teaspoon thyme
1 bay leaf
1 tablespoon butter
Buttered noodles or parsley buttered red potatoes, at serving
    time.

On high heat setting, sauté bacon until crisp and rendered. Remove bacon pieces from skillet and reserve on a paper plate. Brown chicken pieces, on all sides, in the hot bacon fat. Remove chicken to a platter and reserve. Turn heat setting down to 300 degrees. Next add pearl onions, whole mushrooms and green onions to skillet. Sauté lightly to caramelize. Remove vegetables from skillet and reserve on a paper plate. Pour off excess drippings, leaving about 2 tablespoons remaining in skillet. Add garlic and flour to skillet. Cook for about 2 minutes, stirring constantly until flour is brown. Lower heat to 250 degrees. Pour in wine and chicken broth. Stir with a whisk and bring back up to a simmer, making a blended sauce. Add back reserved bacon, chicken pieces and vegetables. Add seasonings of salt, pepper, thyme and bay leaf. Cover and simmer until chicken is tender, about 30 to 40 minutes, or until juice from chicken runs clear. Remove bay leaf from sauce. Stir in 1 pat of butter to "finish" sauce. Serve with lightly buttered, wide flat noodles or parsley buttered boiled potatoes.

Secrets for Success:

Browning and caramelizing everything in bacon fat, before the simmering process, makes for a deeply-rich sauce. This is one case when chicken and red wine truly do go together.

Bonus Recipe: Chicken Chasseur-Style

Thicken and flavor sauce in above recipe with 1 mini can of tomato paste. Voila! Chicken Chasseur!

Chicken with Braised Grape Sauce

Light and easy, this chicken recipe makes an elegant dinner. The nutty flavor of the wild rice contrasted with the sweet flavor of the grapes is a perfect match, when trio-ed with white chicken meat.

6 boneless, skinless chicken breasts
Salt to taste
Freshly grated nutmeg
2 tablespoons butter
1 tablespoon vegetable oil
1 to 2 tablespoons orange marmalade
1 to 2 scallions diced, including tops
A pinch of tarragon, crushed between fingers
A pinch of white pepper
½ cup white wine (water or chicken broth)
1 cup seedless green grapes (or canned grapes, drained)
¼ cup heavy cream
Wild rice at serving time

Season chicken breasts lightly with a sprinkling of salt and nutmeg. Heat oil and butter on medium-high heat setting. Lightly brown chicken breasts in the hot skillet. Add marmalade, scallion, tarragon, white pepper and wine. Cover, reduce heat and simmer for 10 to 15 minutes. Add grapes, add back cover, and simmer 10 to 15 minutes more, or until chicken is cooked through. Add more wine, water, or chicken broth as/and if necessary. When chicken is done, remove to a warm platter and hold until serving time... Stir in heavy cream to blend and continue heating to reduce sauce slightly.

Drizzle sauce over chicken and serve with wild rice. (See page 87 for instructions on cooking and steaming wild rice.)

Secrets for Success:

A delicate touch is required for this dish. Don't over season. Let each ingredient speak for itself—bringing out the subtle flavors of nutmeg, marmalade, tarragon and grapes.

Chicken Cozumel with Rice Tampico

Many years ago, on a little island, on a trip to the Yucatan I was treated to this exotic meal. This recipe is written to serve 4 to 6.

Chicken:
1 fryer chicken, cut up
Canola oil to cover bottom of pan
1 tablespoon butter
2 to 3 tomatoes, seeded and cut up
2 cloves garlic, mashed and minced
1 zucchini, peel left on, sliced
1 package sliced mushrooms
1 small can garbanzo beans
Sea salt and black pepper, to taste
Water as/and if necessary
Rice:
1 cup long grain rice
2 cups chicken broth
1 additional tomato, chopped
1 tablespoon minced onion
Dash cumin
Dash sea salt
Sliced banana for garnish

Sauté chicken fryer pieces in hot oil and butter until golden. Add tomatoes and crush into skillet to make sauce. Cover. Lower heat setting and simmer until chicken is tender and cooked through, about 35 minutes. Half-way through cooking time add in garlic, zucchini, mushrooms, and garbanzo beans. Adjust with sea salt and pepper to taste. Replace cover and continue simmering. During cooking time add water as/and if necessary. After the 35 minutes, remove chicken from skillet and hold tented with foil. Add long grain rice to skillet and stir into pan juices coating well. Add chicken broth, additional tomato, onion, cumin and additional sea salt. Lay chicken back on top and replace cover. Simmer on low heat setting about 25 minutes more until rice is tender and fluffy. Do not stir. Just before serving garnish with sliced banana (this is a must) and serve directly from skillet. Further authenticate the meal with a side of warmed tortillas. Follow with a refreshing dessert of coconut ice cream and sliced tropical fruit.

Secrets for Success:

In the dead of winter, when I need a little pick me up, I pull out this recipe and am instantly transported back to that Mexican patio, where the Chef presented us with his specialty dish... suddenly dinner becomes a "mini vacation" all over again.

Aunt Joan's Costa del Sol Chicken with Shrimp

Aunt Joan traveled the world, collecting recipes on every trip. Once home, an accomplished cook, she would replicate the tastes she loved from her travels.

8 chicken pieces of your choice
Dredging flour, seasoned with salt and pepper
2 tablespoons olive oil
2 tablespoons butter
12 pearl onions
¼ cup diced green pepper, that has been ribbed and seeded
1 cup well drained, quartered Italian tomatoes
¾ cup pitted black olives
1/8 teaspoon of allspice
Salt and pepper to taste
1 cup dry vermouth (or water)
1 cup sautéed, sliced mushrooms
2 to 3 peeled, large raw shrimp per person
Cooked rice, at serving time

Bring olive oil and butter up to temperature in skillet. Dredge chicken pieces in seasoned flour to lightly coat. Sauté chicken 15 minutes, until golden. Add pearl onions through vermouth. Cover, turn down temperature, and simmer 30 minutes. Add sautéed mushrooms and raw shrimp to mixture in skillet. Cover and simmer an additional 7 to 8 minutes, or until shrimp are just cooked through. Serve with steamed rice.

Secrets for Success:

A magnificent dish when company comes to dinner—pearl onions, allspice and large shrimp are musts. Add shrimp last, being careful not to overcook.

Shrimp Jo Ann, Scampi-Style

My sister-in-law, Jo Ann and I used to experiment with this dish when we vacationed in Florida. By-passing the expensive restaurants, we would go to the local seafood market and splurge on the jumbo, fresh shrimp, available that day—We would return back to our beach-cottage to serve up this quickly-cooked, savory, luxuriant meal (minus the lines and crowded restaurants) to all that were anxiously waiting for us. After dinner, we would take a moon-lit walk on the beach, to walk off our meal and 'chalk up' another culinary success. Although I now use flash-frozen shrimp from my mid-western market—and no longer have a beach to walk on, I am forever transported back to those fun-filled vacations in Florida...when we indulgently feasted with family and friends...

Olive oil just to cover bottom of pan
1 to 2 tablespoons butter
2 tablespoons minced onion or shallots
1 tablespoon, freshly minced parsley
Jarred, minced garlic to taste (I like to be heavy on the garlic.)
At least 1 pound freshly caught shrimp, shelled and de-veined,
   or use flash-frozen fresh shrimp thawed according to package
   instructions and patted dry
A shot glass of cooking vermouth (optional)
2 tablespoons freshly squeezed lemon juice
Salt and pepper to taste
Additional lemon wedges, to pass at serving time

Heat oil and butter on medium-high heat setting. Add onion or shallot, and parsley to skillet, cooking for just a minute or two, to soften. Add shrimp and garlic to skillet and sauté quickly until shrimp are pink, opaque and tender. Be careful not to over cook shrimp (cooking time will be very fast—maybe 5 to 6 minutes). Reduce heat setting and add optional vermouth if you wish, cooking only a minute more. Squeeze on lemon juice.

Adjust with salt and pepper to taste. Serve immediately with pan juices drizzled over all. Add wonderful bread and a nice salad to complete the meal. Serve additional lemon wedges on the side.

Secrets for Success:

Simple... quick... uncomplicated... let the ingredients 'speak for themselves'. And for heavens sake, don't skimp on the garlic!

Sautéing garlic: Sautéing minced garlic needs to be done with a watchful eye. Burnt garlic turns very bitter and will ruin any dish. If you burn it, clean out the pan and start over again...there is no salvaging burnt garlic. Often it is wise to add garlic during last part of sautéing process or with the addition of other foods, as it can turn from golden brown to burnt at the blink of an eye when cooked alone.

Suzi's Salmon Patties

Once in a while, nothing beats a good salmon patty! My friend Suzi makes the best! This recipe makes 6 to 8 patties.

1 (14.75 ounce) can Red Sockeye Salmon, drained (Suzi
  suggests Rubensteins®)
1 medium onion, grated
¼ cup Italian seasoned bread crumbs
1 egg
1 tablespoon sour cream
Salt and pepper, to taste
Matzo meal, for dredging
Vegetable cooking oil

Flake and mash salmon. Add remaining ingredients, except for matzo meal and mix well. Heat oil in skillet. While oil is heating, form patties in your hands and lay on waxed paper. Press matzo meal into both sides to coat. Place patties in skillet and sauté until nicely browned on both sides and heated through. Drain on paper toweling before serving.

Secrets for Success

Use a good quality canned salmon and seasoned breadcrumbs. Don't overwork the patties as you form them.

Crab Delights Fettuccini

From the Koopmann Kitchen comes a delightful dish for a special occasion for 4.

6 ounces fettuccine, cooked al dente
¼ cup butter
2 cloves garlic, minced
1 cup half-and-half cream
1 (8 –ounce) package Louis Kemp Crab Delights®
1/8 teaspoon white pepper
½ cup grated Parmesan cheese

Cook fettuccine according to package instructions, drain and reserve. Heat butter, along with minced garlic, on a medium heat setting until melted and foamy and just turning gently brown. Be careful not to scorch garlic. Add half-and-half, Crab Delights® and pepper. Heat just until mixture is warmed through and begins to bubble. Stir in Parmesan cheese for 1 minute. Turn off heat setting and add cooked fettuccine to skillet and toss to incorporate all. Serve immediately. Pass additional Parmesan cheese if desired.

Secrets for Success:

Garlic, butter and half-and-half make for a very rich Alfredo-style sauce. Using white pepper adds a sophisticated touch.

Que es Eso?

Literally translated "What is It?"—it is delicious; I can vouch for that. This recipe is replicated from a dish served in the Zona Rosa, Mexico city. This recipe is written to serve 4 and needs to be accompanied with a salsa of choice.

4 pieces hardened Chihuahua cheese (find in Mexican market or good cheese-specialty shop)
Non-stick cooking spray, or a little cooking oil
Fresh salsa or Salsa Verde

Cut cheese into 4 (1¼ -inch thick) pieces, each about the size of a chop of meat. Spray skillet with non-stick cooking spray and bring up to medium temperature. "Grill" cheese quickly on both sides, just until heated through and starting to soften, but still holds shape. Pour on Salsa Verde, heat another minute or so, and serve immediately. Makes a great appetizer served with warmed tortillas; or a light meatless dinner accompanied with a salad and crusty bread. Allow 1 piece per person.
Serve with garnishes of Salsa Verde, (see recipe on next page).

Salsa Verde

4 tomatillos, peeled of papery skin and chopped in blender
½ cup water
2 hot chilies, seeded and chopped
2 green onions, including tops, chopped
4 sprigs cilantro (flat parsley), chopped

Blend all to a pesto-type consistency in blender or food processor. Serve sauce over sautéed "almost-to-melty" cheese. If you can't find tomatillos, don't let that stop you from enjoying this intriguing dish. A traditional salsa will yield almost the same effect—make your own favorite recipe, or buy jarred.

Secrets for Success:

Utilize ethnic markets in your city to find unusual ingredients to replicate favorite recipes from a wonderful vacation. We have become so cosmopolitan these days that with a little effort we can find just about any ingredient we need to build an ethnic taste in our own kitchens. I have been fortunate to do much traveling around this country and the world—and I find it fun to try to replicate dishes I have been introduced to during my travels. Take the time to discover the old fashioned butcher shops, ethnic bakeries and intriguing specialty shops and aromatic-spice shops in your area. —Even if you don't end up incorporating some of these newly discovered treasures into your family's menu, the visit itself is worth the experience!

Saganaki
(Sautéed Greek Cheese)

I was privileged to work in a Greek restaurant for many years, and ended up flaming and serving many a Saganaki. I owe this recipe to Honey and Nick, Tom and Todd, for introducing me to this wonderful Greek dish...Although this isn't quite the way they make it at the Fireplace Inn, it comes in a close second! Ahhhh...that I could have Honey cook me up one right now...Use 1 generous piece of cheese per serving.

Kasseri cheese, cut into individual, thick, chop-size pieces
  (allow 1 piece per person)
Egg-wash (i.e. 1egg beaten with 1 to 2 tablespoons water for
  dipping)
Flour, for dredging
Olive oil (or clarified butter) to cover bottom of pan
1 shot-glass brandy (or ouzo)
Juice from 2 lemon wedges (per slice of cheese)
Good bread, at serving time

Bring olive oil (or clarified butter, see page 163) up to medium-hot temperature in skillet. Cut cheese into chop-size pieces. Dip into egg wash to coat. Then roll egg-washed cheese in flour to coat well. Sauté quickly until golden brown both sides (about 3 minutes per side), or until cheese is softened but not quite runny. Carefully pour on 1 shot-glass of brandy (or ouzo) and ignite. Douse flames with juice freshly squeezed from lemon wedges. Serve immediately. Eat the cheese with a knife and fork like a chop, and accompany with good bread for dipping into all the buttery juices. Although usually served as an appetizer, this dish makes a nice light meatless dinner accompanied with a salad and the bread.

Secrets for Success:

If you don't have access to Kasseri cheese, Pecorino Romano runs a close second. Or visit a good cheese-specialty shop to find just what you need—ask their recommendation for a very hard cheese that can be cut into chop-size pieces from a wheel of cheese suitable for Saganaki.

Bush's® Cajun Red Beans and Rice

*This dish hails from the kitchens of BUSH'S BEST ®
beans. Creole in taste, it quickly cooks up for a warming
dinner for 4—a great dish when chili just won't do.*

3 tablespoons vegetable oil
1 green bell pepper, chopped
1 medium onion, chopped
3 garlic cloves, chopped
3 stalks celery, chopped
1 pound Andouille sausage, sliced (or similar smoked sausage)
2 (16 ounce) cans BUSH'S BEST® red (or light red) kidney
  beans
3 tablespoons Creole-style seasoning
Hot cooked (white or brown) rice, at serving time.

Heat vegetable oil on a 325 to 350-degree setting. Sauté
bell pepper, onion, garlic and celery until tender. Add
sausage slices and cook until done. Pour in red beans
and season with Creole seasoning. Simmer for an
additional 5 minutes, or until all is heated through. Serve
over hot cooked rice.

Secrets for Success:

Andouille sausage is a spicy, Spanish sausage that can be
readily found in today's market. I have found that
pepperoni can be substituted in a pinch. You want this to
be a spicy dish, counteracted by the blandness of the rice.
Serve with a bottle of hot sauce (for the adventuresome)

on the side. A dollop of cold, rich sour cream also makes a great garnish against the Creole flavors and spicy sausage. Add a salad and some crusty bread and you are 'ready to go.'

Omit the meat altogether, add some more veggies, and you have a great base for a vegetarian-style meal.

Individual, little side cups of lemon sherbet or sorbet served alongside would add a cooling treat for the palate as you enjoy this Cajun dish.

Gary Fairchild's Brunch-Style Chicken Livers

For many years it was my holiday tradition to host a Christmas Day Brunch. I would set the table with my mother's china and finest crystal, polish up the silver and open the doors to as many of my friends who could attend. Each guest would bring the fixings for and/or cook a special dish to add to the table. My kitchen would be filled with "many cooks" on that special day...and the resultant table would be quite an ensemble. Gary Fairchild would always make this fabulous dish. It is ever so basic (measurements don't really matter) but ever so good (another example of simple can be sublime).

At least 1 pound fresh chicken livers, rinsed and cut in half
1 onion, chopped
1 package sliced mushrooms
½ stick butter
Salt and pepper to taste
A little Sherry or wine
Toasted and buttered English muffins, at serving time

On a medium-high heat setting, bring butter up to temperature. Start by sautéing onion to soften and then adding mushrooms for a minute or two. Add in chicken livers and continue sautéing until browned, about 4 to 5 minutes. Do not over cook. Add Sherry or wine and heat for another minute or two. Serve as a brunch accompaniment to scrambled eggs and toasted English muffins, or pile onto buttered toast points as an entrée.

Secrets for Success:

This dish requires a watchful eye. Chicken livers cook up very fast and you don't want them to dry out and become chewy. They will be fully cooked before you know it.

Bourbon Steak

Hearty and sauce-y, this is a great way to serve filet mignon for 4 special guests.

4 generous cuts of beef tenderloin (filet mignon)
4 tablespoons butter (preferably clarified, see next page)
Salt and pepper to taste
2 teaspoons Worcestershire sauce
½ cup warm bourbon, in a long handled pot or ladle
1 cup brown sauce (use good quality jarred)
4 teaspoons Dijon-style mustard
4 teaspoons sour cream
Hot buttered noodles for serving

On a medium to high heat setting melt butter in skillet, being careful not to burn. When butter begins to sizzle and foam, quickly sauté steaks, about 3 to 5 minutes per side, or according to doneness that you like. Do not over cook. Lightly season to taste with salt, pepper and the Worcestershire sauce. Very carefully pour bourbon over steaks and ignite. Bourbon is very flammable—NEVER, ever pour it directly from the bottle! Cook until flame dies down. Transfer steaks to warm platter and continue with sauce. Add the cup of brown sauce and the mustard, stirring into skillet just until heated. Stir in sour cream just until heated. Do not let sauce boil. Pour sauce over steaks. Serve with buttered noodles.

When using butter alone for high- heat sautéing, clarifying it first helps prevent burning.

Clarifying Butter

Clarified butter is unsalted butter that has been melted and then the milk-solids have been removed, leaving a clear golden liquid also known as "Drawn Butter"— something that we are all familiar with in the little dipping cups on our seafood and lobster platters. However this butter is also good for more than just dipping! Clarified butter is very good for sautéing and pan frying at high temperatures, because it has a higher heat tolerance and doesn't burn as easily. So if you are not mixing butter with oil for high-heat cooking, best to clarify it first.

To clarify butter, melt at least 2 sticks of butter in a small saucepan, over low heat until it begins to bubble. Simmer for about 2 minutes, while the butter separates. Remove from heat and let stand about 10 minutes. Milk solids will separate-out and sink to the bottom. Carefully pour the "clarified" portion into a container. Discard the milk solids that have sunk to the bottom of the pot. Clarified butter will keep, tightly covered, for up to a month in the refrigerator. Use it whenever the recipe calls for frying and sautéing with butter, especially at high temperatures.

Beef Medallions with Cognac Sauce

Shallots, cognac and heavy cream make this truly an elegant entrée. Use 1 cut of filet mignon per person.

1 generous cut of beef tenderloin steak (filet mignon) per person
Salt and pepper to taste
4 tablespoons butter (see clarified butter, page 163)
½ cup cognac or fine brandy, in a ladle or long handled pot
¼ cup diced shallots
1 teaspoon packed brown sugar
½ cup canned chicken broth
½ cup canned beef broth
¼ cup whipping cream

Bring butter up to temperature on a high setting, being careful not to burn. While butter is melting season steaks on both sides with salt and pepper. Quickly sauté steaks in heated butter (according to your liking)—about 3 to 5 minutes per side. Do not over cook. From a ladle carefully pour on ½ cup cognac and ignite. NEVER, ever pour flammable liquors straight from the bottle! Remove steaks to warm platter and tent with foil, or hold in warm oven. Continue with sauce. Add shallots to skillet and cook for a minute, stirring up any flavorful bits in pan. Add brown sugar and stir. Add broths and stir to heat. Simmer sauce for a few minutes to reduce. Turn down skillet to lowest heat setting and lastly stir in heavy cream—do not let sauce boil after adding cream. Return steaks to pan to re-warm if needed, and spoon over with sauce. Serve immediately.

Secrets for Success:

Shallots are a must for this dish. If you are not familiar with them, they can be found in the produce section of your market, usually sold in little mesh bags. Shallots are a mild member of the onion family and look like small, papery sheathed bulbs, with kind of a purplish color. They are valued in cooking for their delicate yet onion-y flavor.

Steak Diane

Spice-y, bold—"Diane" knew what she was doing when she invented this recipe! Use 1 cut of filet mignon per person.

1 generous cut of beef tenderloin (filet mignon) per person
Coarsely-ground, mixed steak seasoning (your choice from the
 spice rack of your market)
Freshly cracked black pepper
¼ teaspoon dry mustard
4 tablespoons butter (see clarified butter, page 163)
The juice squeezed from 1 lemon
1 teaspoon Worcestershire sauce
2 teaspoons snipped chives
1 additional pat of butter

On a plate make a "dry rub" by mixing generous amounts of steak-seasoning-spice-mix, freshly cracked pepper and a little dry mustard, for extra added zip. Dredge steak on both sides in the mix, and press mix into the meat, coating well. Let steaks stand for a few minutes to absorb the dry-rub flavors. Bring butter up to high temperature, being careful not to burn, and quickly sauté steaks on both sides—about 3 to 5 minutes per side (for rare to medium rare respectively). Remove steaks to warm platter and reserve. Squeeze the juice of a lemon into the skillet juices and add the Worcestershire and chives. Stir to get up any flavorful bits in pan. Stir in 1 final pat of butter to "finish" sauce. Drizzle over reserved steaks and serve immediately. Add a baked potato and a salad (from Beyond the Pan section) to complete the meal.

Secrets for Success:

Filet mignon is perhaps the tenderest cut of beef you can purchase. Granted it seems expensive, but there is absolutely no waste and you are not paying for fat or bone. On its own, it doesn't have the flavor of 'beefier' steaks such as T-bone, sirloin, rib-eye, and New York strip (each marbled with their fat or flavored with their bone). Thusly, it becomes the perfect candidate to receive a luscious sauce (as in this, and the previous two recipes). Cook it quick—3 to 5 minutes per side (taking into account that steak will still "cook" a little more while holding or "standing" as you make the sauce).—I personally think it is a crime to cook such an extravagant steak to well done, but in the end I will leave that up to you...

Steak Donna

"Not to be outdone by Diane" (previous recipe)...my friend Donna invented her own fabulous way to serve steak.

1 generous cut of beef tenderloin (filet mignon) per person
2 tablespoons unsalted butter, and additional if necessary when making sauce
½ cup finely diced white-part of scallions; reserve green tops for garnish
½ cup white wine
1 cup heavy cream
2 dried chipotle peppers, reconstituted in boiling water until soft, then finely diced
1 tablespoon liquid reserved from chipotle pepper process
¼ cup sour cream, or additional to taste if needed
Salt and freshly ground pepper to taste
Reserved green tops from the scallions, sliced very thin in julienne for garnish

In a small sauce pan, or using a microwave and a microwave-safe dish, re-hydrate the 2 chipotle peppers in a little boiling water until softened and tender. Cool, drain and finely dice peppers, reserving the liquid separately. Set both dice and liquid aside. Meanwhile, bring butter up to high temperature, being careful not to burn, and quickly sauté steaks on both sides (at a 350 degree setting)—about 3 to 5 minutes per side (for rare to medium rare respectively). Do not crowd pan. Remove steaks to warm platter and reserve while making sauce. Lower heat setting to low-medium and add additional butter to pan if needed. Stir in diced white part of scallions and gently sauté until softened but not brown, about 3 minutes. Add wine and simmer to reduce, stirring all the while, about another 5 minutes. At this point add the heavy cream and the finely diced chipotles (see Donna's optional secret for success below). Once the cream has been added never let the sauce come to a boil again. Gently simmer to reduce and thicken. Stir in 1 tablespoon reserved chipotle liquid and the sour cream. Season with salt and pepper to taste. If your sauce is too spicy, add a little more sour cream to adjust flavor to your liking. Add steaks back to skillet, making sure both steaks and sauce are warmed through. Spoon sauce onto each serving plate and place steak on top of sauce. Garnish with an "architectural "sprinkling of very thinly sliced scallion tops for added color and contrast. Serve immediately.

Secrets for Success:

To make the sauce ultra-creamy and smooth, Donna runs the diced peppers along with the heavy cream through a blender or food processor before adding to the skillet. This makes for an elegant sauce, but is totally optional. The sauce is good either way, and this extra step is up to you. If you are not a steak eater, this chipotle-cream sauce works well on a substitution of chicken breasts in place of the steaks. Either way it's a winner!

"Make-It-a-Date" Steaks with Red Wine for Two

Red meat, red wine, simple in preparation—this is a man's dinner. Make a date. Invite your 'hubbie' or significant-other into the kitchen and cook together. Then sit down over candle light to enjoy your feast.

2 at least 1-inch thick New York strip steaks
Salt and freshly cracked pepper
4 tablespoons butter, divided
¼ cup minced shallots
½ cup good red wine, such as Burgundy, Merlot, or Cabernet;
   reserve the rest to accompany meal
Additional salt and freshly cracked pepper
The divided out pat of butter

Trim excess fat from steaks and reserve. On a medium-high heat setting melt a little of the trimmed fat to cover bottom of skillet, discarding any excess. (This is basically called "rendering"). Sauté steaks to your liking in the hot, rendered fat. Turn once and season with salt and pepper. Continue sautéing to reach your liking of doneness. Remove steaks to warm serving plates. Add 3 tablespoons of butter and minced shallots to skillet, stirring to bring up any flavorful bits in pan. Cook until shallots are translucent. Add wine and cook to reduce by half. Season with additional salt and pepper to taste. Swirl in final tablespoon of butter to "finish" sauce. Spoon pan-sauce over steaks and serve immediately. Accompany with a glass of the good remaining wine (it has now had time to aerate). Add crusty French bread to complete the meal.

Secrets for Success:

Salt and Pepper: Every kitchen should have a good pepper mill. There is nothing better than freshly ground pepper. Pepper looses its punch after being ground and stored in those little jars on the spice shelf at the supermarket. Next time you fill your pepper grinder, try a mixed batch of colorful pepper corns for a culinary treat. Grind it fresh at every meal. Salt is also a matter of consideration and personal preference. There are kosher salts, coarse salt, salt grinders, salt shakers, individual salt cellars with little spoons, table salt in tubs, iodized salt, lite-salt, sea salt, low-salt, no salt-salt substitute—the list of options seems endless and offers a great variety for us to choose from.

Chef's Steak-Doneness Guide—You can test for doneness by pressing on the steak with your finger. Rare will offer a slight resistance, much like pressing the softly-relaxed palm of your hand at the cushiony-base-pad of your thumb and palm. Medium-rare offers more resistance when touched—springing back lightly, like the feeling you get when you press your now slightly flexed hand. Medium-well (and Well-done) get increasingly resistant—much like feeling a well-extended and stretched palm and pad, which have now become tight and very springy. Try this test a few times and you will get to know "the feel" of the doneness you like—and you can omit cutting into the steak and letting out all the good juices before it's done.

Lamb with Snow Peas

When I was living in Madison, WI and my then-husband was in graduate school—we would occasionally entertain his professors. I would cook this dish...and "I'd like to think that 'my cooking' played a part in the attainment of his degree!" That was so many years ago and I still make this dish today when company comes to dinner. This recipe serves 6 as deliciously today as it did so many years ago.

1 pound lamb, cubed
3 tablespoons butter (use clarified butter, see page 163)
1 large onion, thinly sliced
½ cup water
1½ teaspoons salt
¼ teaspoon pepper
¼ cup freshly squeezed lemon juice
2 pounds fresh mushrooms, sliced
1 can water chestnuts, drained and sliced thin
A generous amount of fresh snow peas (or can use a package
   of frozen and thawed, if you can't find fresh)
Cooked white or brown rice, at serving time

In your heated skillet, sauté lamb in butter until browned, being careful not to burn. Push meat to the side and add onion, cooking until softened. Turn down heat setting, add water and stir all together. Cover and simmer gently for 30 minutes. Add more water if necessary during cooking process. Add salt, pepper, lemon juice and mushrooms. Simmer for 15 minutes more. Add water chestnuts and cook for 2 minutes. Add snow peas, cover once again and cook just until snow peas are crisp-crunchy tender. Serve with hot cooked rice.

Secrets for Success:

You want your lamb succulent and tender—and the water chestnuts and snow peas cooked yet crisp. The lemon juice just "makes the dish"—giving it a fresh, clean, straight-forward taste. This is one of the rare times that I don't include garlic with my lamb.

Veal Stroganoff

Delicate, rich yet subtle—veal, mushrooms and yogurt make a nice combination—and so easy to cook up in the skillet.

1½ pounds veal cutlet, cut into ¼ -inch strips
½ teaspoon salt
¼ teaspoon pepper
4 tablespoons butter
2 additional tablespoons butter
¼ cup diced onion
4 ounces sliced mushrooms
1 clove garlic, mashed and minced
3 tablespoons flour
1 can chicken broth
2 tablespoons brandy, optional
½ pint plain yogurt
Hot buttered noodles at serving time

Season veal strips with salt and pepper and sauté quickly in 4 tablespoons hot butter. Remove from skillet and hold on warm platter tented with foil. Add additional butter to pan juices in skillet. Add onion, mushrooms and garlic, and sauté a few minutes. Stir in flour to make a roux. Stir in chicken broth and cook to thicken and heat thoroughly. Add back veal to skillet and simmer until heated through. Reduce heat, stir in brandy and then yogurt. Do not boil after yogurt is added. When all is heated through, serve with hot buttered noodles on the side.

Secrets for Success:

Although expensive, veal can add a nice variety to your cooking repertoire once in a while. Using veal in a stroganoff, accompanied with noodles, is a great way to "stretch" your dollar and create a fabulous dinner. If you don't want to use brandy, you can substitute a teaspoon of Maggi® seasoning sauce or Kitchen Bouguet®.

Veal Marsala for Two *(or Eight)*

This recipe is written as a special dinner for 2, but can be expanded to serve as many as 8. (I have listed the increased amounts to make this dish for 8 in parenthesis.)

2 veal cutlets, pounded to ¼-inch thickness	*(8 cutlets)*
½ cup flour	*(1 cup)*
½ cup grated Parmesan cheese	*(3/4 cup)*
1 teaspoon salt	*(2 teaspoons)*
¼ teaspoon pepper	*(1 teaspoon)*
2 tablespoons olive oil *(add additional, sautéing meat in batches)*	
2 tablespoons butter *(add additional, sautéing meat in batches)*	
2 additional tablespoons butter	*(3 tablespoons)*
¼ box sliced mushrooms	*(1 whole box)*
Salt and pepper to taste	*(½ teaspoon each)*
Dash of cayenne	*(2 dashes)*
¼ cup canned beef stock	*(1 can)*
1 teaspoon cornstarch, softened in water	*(1 tablespoon)*
¼ cup Marsala (or Madeira wine)	*(3/4 cup)*

Between layers of waxed paper or plastic wrap, pound cutlets to ¼-inch thickness. Mix flour, Parmesan cheese, salt and pepper together in a pie plate. Dredge and coat veal pieces thoroughly with flour mixture. Heat olive oil and butter on 325 to 350-degree heat setting. Sauté veal quickly on both sides and remove to warm platter. Add additional butter to skillet and sauté mushrooms, adding seasonings of salt, pepper and cayenne. Stir in beef stock, then softened cornstarch, and then Marsala (or Madeira) to make sauce. Stir and heat thoroughly. Pour pan sauce over veal and serve. Accompany with buttered noodles.

Secrets for Success:

Both Marsala and/or Madeira have a sweet rich flavor all their own. They are excellent for making deep rich sauces and go great with veal. When selecting your wine for this dish, choose either Marsala or Madeira, as their flavor cannot be replicated by other red wines, and one or the other is necessary for this recipe.

Veal Scaloppini

This is one of my absolutely favorite dishes—and so easy and quick to make, with such elegant results—a true dish for company or a special occasion.

1 pound veal, use tender cutlets pounded to ¼ -inch thickness
  for scaloppini
2 tablespoons butter
2 tablespoons olive oil
Flour for dredging
Salt and pepper to taste
½ cup chicken broth or beef broth
A splash of white wine (optional)
Juice from a fresh lemon
1 tablespoon freshly minced parsley
1 to 2 tablespoons jarred capers, drained
Lemon wedges, at serving time

Make sure the veal meat has been pounded thin, into "escalope-style" pieces. Dredge meat in flour to coat, shaking off any excess. Bring butter and olive oil up to temperature on 325 to 350 heat setting. Sauté veal until golden brown, turning as needed, to brown both sides. Season with salt and pepper to taste. Lower heat setting and add broth and wine. Loosen tasty bits from bottom of skillet. Continue to cook a few more minutes to reduce sauce, blend flavors, and finish cooking the veal. (Total cooking time about 12 minutes.) Turn off heat setting completely. Squeeze in the juice of a lemon, sprinkle on the parsley and garnish each "scaloppini" with capers. Serve immediately on warmed plates with pan-sauces divided over each serving. Pass extra wedges of lemon.

Use good quality veal, pounded very thin and cooked quickly. Fresh lemon juice and capers are a must. I like to take my scaloppini just "over the top" by adding a fried egg per each serving, as suggested below.

Veal Scaloppini a la Holstein

1 egg for each serving in above recipe
butter, to fry the eggs

In a separate pan fry-up the number of eggs needed (using 1 per serving). Eggs should be nicely fried "sunny-side-up" with the yolk just softly-firm, but not hard. Be careful not to over cook the eggs. Place an egg on each veal serving, then garnish with the parsley and capers.

Secrets for Success:

Use a delicate touch when frying the eggs for this recipe. You want them to be "just perfect." And don't skimp on the capers! This is one dish you have to enjoy, guilt- and diet-free...

"Veau de Julia"

I have been making this dish for years. Deceptively elegant, it makes a splendid dinner for 6. I have entered this dish in my book in honor of Julia Child--pioneer and 'free spirit' in the cooking world of TV shows and specialty cookbooks. Julia taught us all to enjoy specialty cooking, without fear of the 'b word' (butter) and without fear of making dishes from scratch, just as our mothers before us... Thank you Julia for introducing me to the perfect world of country French cooking! My sister and I spent hours competing for the best interpretations of your recipes...I won on this one!

1 (3 to 4 pound) boneless veal roast
2 tablespoons Canola oil
2 tablespoons butter
3 carrots, 1/8 -inch dice
2 onions, 1/8 -inch dice
½ teaspoon salt
¼ teaspoon white peppper
4 black peppercorns
2 whole cloves
1/4 cup fresh, minced parsley
1 to 2 bay leaves
A pinch of thyme
A pinch of herbs Provencale
1/3 to 1/2 cup Madeira wine
1 cup beef stock or broth
1 tablespoon cornstarch
2 tablespoons additional Madeira wine
2 tablespoons butter

Bring oil and butter up to temperature of 350 degrees. Brown roast on all sides. Remove from skillet. Add carrots and onion to skillet and sauté in pan juices 10 minutes. Return roast to skillet. Season with salt and pepper and spread half of the vegetables over top of roast. Add parsley, bay leaf, thyme, herbs Provencale, cloves and peppercorns, and then Madeira wine. "Tent" the roast with a covering of foil. Then place cover on skillet. Simmer (doubly-covered) at 325 degrees, 30 to 40 minutes per pound. Remove roast to warm platter and keep warm. Discard bay leaf, pepper corns and cloves from skillet. Add beef stock or broth to skillet. Boil 5 minutes, getting up all the wonderful bits in bottom of pan. Soften cornstarch in Madeira wine and add mixture to skillet. Simmer and stir until thickened. To "finish" sauce swirl in 2 pats of butter just until melted. Serve sauce in a warm gravy boat along with slices of roast and the addition of mashed potatoes or parsley buttered new potatoes. I cannot begin to tell you how luxurious and delicious this dinner is!

Secrets for Success:

'Tenting' the roast with foil before adding the skillet cover captures and re-circulates the steam down into the meat—making for a most tender roast. Finishing the sauce with a swirl of butter adds ultimate richness to the sauce. Rich Madeira wine is an absolute must for this dish—no other will do.

Lobster Paella-Style

Okay—this recipe is extravagant, I admit—but I thought it might be fun to end this chapter with a very indulgent dinner for a special occasion. Amounts used will depend on the size of your electric skillet...and the 'market price' of lobster!

1 whole lobster, semi-cooked and left in shell
Olive oil
1 chicken thigh per person, with skin and cut into halves
  (washed and patted dry)
Salt and pepper
3 to 4 tomatoes (halve, squeeze out seeds, and dice)
1 red bell pepper, ribbed, seeded and roughly diced
2 to 3 garlic cloves, minced
2 cups long grain rice
4 cups hot water or hot chicken broth (formula is: 1 part rice to 2
  parts liquid)
A slight pinch of saffron threads, that have been added to and
  softened in the heated water or broth (this releases the color
  and flavor of the expensive saffron)
Fresh clams and/or mussels, in their shell

Poach whole lobster for only a couple of minutes in boiling water. (It will finish cooking when added to paella.) Remove and drain. Cut tail into chunks, leaving shell on. Be sure to break off claws, and include all legs (even the little ones) and any other usable parts, with their shell Crack serving-size pieces and leave all in the shell. Set aside. (Discard remaining, unusable lobster.) In your preheated skillet, set on a medium-high heat, brown and cook chicken-thigh pieces in olive oil, seasoning with salt and pepper to taste (about 10 to 12 minutes). Remove and set aside. Add diced tomato, red bell pepper and garlic to skillet, and sauté to soften vegetables and meld flavors (about 5 minutes). Add rice and stir to coat in pan juices. Add back chicken to skillet. Pour in heated saffron-water (or heated saffron-broth). Cover and cook until rice is tender and water is becoming absorbed (about 20 minutes). When rice is getting toward done, place the reserved lobster pieces (shell and all) and the fresh clams and/or mussels (in their shells) on top. Cover and continue cooking (about 15 minutes more) until dish becomes semi-dry, lobster is cooked through, and clams (and/or mussels) have opened. Discard any clams or mussels that haven't opened during cooking (as these are not safe to eat). Serve from the pan, making sure each serving has a representative mixture of all ingredients. Add a crusty bread to complete the meal. Dive in and enjoy. Have plenty of napkins or finger towels on hand.

Secrets for Success:

The keys to this dish are the saffron threads (you need just a touch) and the lobster, cracked and left in its shell. If you don't want to fiddle with a whole lobster, substitute the equivalent in tails (use 2 or 3 depending on size) cut into chunks, shell left on. The amounts of ingredients used are totally up to you, and will be ultimately determined by the size of your electric skillet and the type of lobster available to you.

Chapter Four:
The Sign of a Good Cook
is a Good Side Dish

Skillet-sides to prepare in your electric skillet

"Behind every entrée there is a good side dish." This chapter is filled with a variety of side dishes to round out your meals. Fried Asparagus to Fried Bananas gives you plenty of suggestions to add variety and vitamins to your menu. Who ever thought veggies could be so good...

The Sign of a Good Cook is a Good Side Dish Index

Glazed Carrots

When my granddaughter wouldn't eat her carrots, I tried fixing them this way (a favorite of mine when I was a child)—and now this vegetable dish has become a favorite part of her meal!

Fresh carrots, washed, peeled and cut into julienne strips
Water for simmering
Butter
Brown sugar

Simmer julienne-d carrots until just-under fully cooked. Drain off water and add carrots back to skillet. Melt butter in skillet, stirring to mix around carrots. Sprinkle on a little brown sugar and continue to heat and stir until sugar melts and carrots become coated and glazed.

Sautéed Garden Parsnips

My Dad used to grow parsnips (amongst the peonies) in our back yard. He'd pick them fresh and cook them up (starchy and sweet) for many a summer dinner.

Fresh parsnips, peeled and cut into very thin julienne strips
Butter (preferably clarified)
Dash of salt and pepper

If you buy your parsnips from the grocery store, be sure to pare off the waxy coating on the outside. (This is used to keep the parsnips fresh during extended storage.) Pare the snips and julienne into very thin strips. Sauté slowly in butter until (about 15 to 20 minutes) until tender and golden brown. Parsnips will be sweet and tender, yet kind of chewy. Season with a little salt and pepper.

Cile's Cauliflower with Brown Butter

My mother-in-law taught me how to make Brown Butter and it remains one of my favorite accents to side dishes today. Old fashioned yet great in flavor, I think most people, today, overlook the rich-flavorful addition of Brown Butter to many a dish. Cile used it mainly on cauliflower, but it has other uses too.

A firm, compact, head of cauliflower, cleaned and left whole
Water
1 stick butter
Dry bread crumbs, to taste
Salt and pepper

In a separate, large pot of boiling water poach the head of cauliflower until fork tender, about 20 minutes. Remove cauliflower, drain and nestle in warm serving bowl. Meanwhile in your skillet, on medium-high to high heat setting melt the stick of butter and cook until gently and richly browned, but not burned, adding in the bread crumbs while cooking. Pour Brown Butter over head of cauliflower. Season lightly with salt and pepper. Serve immediately.

Secrets for Success:

Brown Butter is so fabulous in flavor and so easy to make.

Bonus Recipe: Browned Butter is excellent on freshly poached Brussels sprouts. (Boil trimmed sprouts to fork tender, drain, and stir into a skillet of browned butter and bread crumbs to coat.)

Brown Butter over Dumplings: Use as a rich-garnish-topping over cooked noodles or cooked dumplings or cooked spaetzle, for a real experience of "comfort food."

Mom's "Next Day" Fried Corn

This is a great way to use up leftover corn on the cob.

Leftover cooked corn on the cob
Butter
Dash of salt and pepper

Standing cobs on end, carefully slice down and around each cob, cutting off kernels with a sharp knife. Discard cobs. Simply sauté the corn kernels in butter until caramelized and gently browned. Corn will be chewy and sweet when done. (Popping sounds will occur in pan as it cooks, although you will not end up with "pop corn"). Salt and pepper to taste.

Sautéed Olives in Wine

This unusual twist to olives can be used as a side dish or an out-of-the-ordinary appetizer for 4 to 6 delighted diners.

2 cups, brine cured black olives, drained
2 tablespoons virgin olive oil
1 cup dry red wine (Use a good drinking wine)
½ teaspoon fennel seeds, crushed to release flavor
3 garlic cloves, crushed
4 to 6 whole black peppercorns, for flavor

Using low-medium heat setting, simmer olives in remaining ingredients for 20 minutes to meld flavors and warm through. Serve warm. Offer remaining wine to accompany dish.

Secrets for Success:

Makes a great side dish along with grilled meats--or a tasty addition to any holiday table.

Park Ridge
Parsnip Patties

Often overlooked as a delectable side dish, my Dad used to grow parsnips every summer and I was introduced to this delicious root vegetable as a child. Parsnips have remained as one of my "comfort foods" to this day.

Fresh parsnips, peeled and cut into chunks
Water
Salt and pepper
Butter
Flour or dry breadcrumbs, for dredging

Prepare parsnips as if you are preparing potatoes for mashing. Boil snips in water until fork-tender-soft and ready for mashing. Drain. With an electric beater, mash until smooth, adding seasonings of salt and pepper and a little butter. Form mashed parsnips into patties. Dredge patties in flour or fine, dry breadcrumbs to coat both sides. Melt butter to cover bottom of skillet. On a medium heat setting, sauté patties until golden brown, both sides and warmed through. Add more butter as necessary. Serve warm.

Secrets for Success:
Store bought parsnips work just as well, so this recipe can be available to you year 'round—Rather intimidating looking, in their waxy covering, it is hard to believe they can be so sweet and delectable. Be sure to remove all outer waxy covering if you are using store bought "snips".

Green Beans Amandine

Jazz up your beans by turning them into Amandine.

Fresh or frozen green beans, French-cut style
Water
Sliced almonds
Butter
Salt and pepper, to taste

Cook French-cut beans in simmering water, just a few minutes until tender. Do not overcook. Drain. Transfer beans to a skillet, in which you have melted and browned the butter with the almonds. Toss to coat. Lightly season with salt and pepper. Serve immediately.

Secrets for Success:

Do not overcook the beans—you want them just fork tender and bright green in color.

Amandine can be used to jazz up any vegetable; do not just reserve this technique for green beans!

Great Aunt Marie's Mushrooms 'n Cream

"Stroganoff" in style, this is a great way to prepare a side of mushrooms.

16 ounces choice, fresh, button mushrooms, whole or halved (depending on size), stems trimmed (or use uniform, thick slices of Portabellas)
3 tablespoons butter
2 tablespoons water
1 cup sour cream
Snipped chives, to taste
Salt, to taste
Paprika, to taste
Dash of Sherry (optional)

Select clean, white, tightly capped mushrooms. Gently brush off any dirt (do not wash) and cut larger mushrooms in half. Trim off tough portion of stems. Heat butter and water in skillet. Add mushrooms and sauté gently for just a few minutes, until tender. Do not over cook. Stir in sour cream and gently cook, until sauce is warmed through and blended to your liking. Season with snipped chives, salt and paprika to taste. Add a dash of Sherry if you wish. Serve as a side dish as an enhancement to grilled meats or baked chicken. Can also serve as a light entrée on buttered toast points, accompanied with a good salad (see "Beyond the Pan" chapter for ideas).

Secrets for Success:

There has been great debate over whether to clean mushrooms by washing or brushing. I prefer brushing—they even make a little brush for this purpose, although a paper towel can do the trick. If you insist on washing your mushrooms, be sure to immediately and totally dry them with paper toweling, as mushrooms absorb water very quickly. When you bring your mushrooms home from the store, be sure to loosen the saran coating on the package before storing in fridge—mushrooms need to "breathe." Discard any dark, withered or slippery mushrooms. Mushrooms are very perishable and must be used within just a few days of purchase. If in doubt discard and buy fresh.

*As a side note: Unless you absolutely! know what you are doing, I would not advise picking and using wild mushrooms!

"Deep Fried" Asparagus

I was never much one for asparagus, until I had it served this way. I guarantee this will be a great deviation from the traditional spring vegetable served with Hollandaise Sauce or Lemon Butter.

Fresh asparagus spears, stalks snapped at their natural
    breaking point
½ pie plate of flour
A little pancake batter, or commercial batter mix, mixed
    according to box instructions
Salt and pepper
Canola cooking oil, to a depth of ¼ to ½ -inch in skillet at 375
    degrees

Trim asparagus by snapping off tough bottoms of stalks. Blanch in boiling water for 3 to 4 minutes to tenderize. Drain and pat dry with paper toweling. (This can be done ahead of time.) Dredge prepared asparagus in flour, then dip into batter mix, one at a time. Slide each stalk into hot skillet of hot oil. Do not crowd skillet. You want oil to remain very hot. "Deep fry" until batter is golden and crisp, and asparagus is tender. Remove with tongs and drain on paper toweling. Sprinkle with salt and pepper while hot. Serve immediately to avoid soggy batter.

Fried Fresh Corn

Get the taste of corn on the cob—without the cob!

1 dozen fresh ears of summer corn, husked and silk removed (I
   like the yellow and white kernelled variety.)
½ stick butter
Salt and freshly cracked black pepper

Standing ears of corn on end, with a sharp knife pare
down the ears, cutting kernels off as close to cob as
possible. Sauté corn in butter on low-medium heat
setting for 5 to 10 minutes, or just until tender and
buttery. Lightly season with salt and pepper. (You can
add a little whole milk or cream, and cook a couple
minutes more to make fresh cream-style-corn of you
wish.)

Secrets for Success:

Use corn within day of purchase. Remove husks and silks
just before cooking, to prevent corn from drying out.
Plump, juicy kernels and freshness are key!

Great Aunt Betty's Asparagus

Great Aunt Betty used to grow beautiful asparagus in her garden—picking it just before dinner time. This is another great way to present asparagus.

Buy tightly-budded green asparagus (or as Aunt Betty used to do, use garden grown)
Salted water
Butter
Breadcrumbs
Lemon slices, for garnish

Select firm, green stalks of asparagus with tight, nicely colored tops. Trim asparagus by "snapping off" bottoms of stalks. (Asparagus stalks have a natural breaking point.) Peel sides of stalks if not young. Stand asparagus upright (you can tie in bundles if you wish) and boil in salted water, with just the tips sticking out. Boil until just fork tender—about 8-12 minutes, depending on size of stalks. Meanwhile brown your butter and bread crumbs in the skillet (see page 190 for Browned Butter). Drain asparagus and transfer to skillet to coat in the browning butter. Hold on warm setting till ready to serve. Serve 5 or 6 stalks per person, on side plates. Garnish each serving with a slice of lemon.

Secrets for Success:

The secret to preparing any vegetable is not to over cook it—taking advantage of its inherent taste, texture and color. Use fresh vegetables whenever possible and use them within a day of purchase or harvesting. Keep your presentation simple, not overpowering.

Stewed Tomato and Zucchini Medley

Not just for pasta sauce—cooked tomatoes make a wonderful side dish, any time of the year!

½ pound young zucchini, sliced
3 tablespoons butter
1 to 2 green onions, including tops, diced
3 to 4 large ripe tomatoes (a good pound's worth), peeled and
  rustically cut into chunks (or can substitute canned peeled
  tomatoes)
¼ cup water, broth or wine
2 to 3 teaspoons sugar (white or brown)
Bread croutons (Cut leftover French bread into ½-inch size
  cubes and toast on cookie sheet in low oven.)
Salt and pepper to taste

On low-medium heat setting, gently sauté zucchini and onions in butter 2 to 3 minutes, for flavor. Add the fresh tomatoes and water (broth or wine). Add a little sugar to taste. Cover skillet and simmer gently until tomatoes are "stewed" and tender, about 10 minutes. (If using canned tomatoes, cooking time may be shorter.) Lightly season with salt and pepper to taste. Lastly stir in toasted croutons. Serve warm in little side bowls.

Secrets for Success:
(As with any vegetable) cooking-timing is key. You want softened, sauce-y tomatoes and zucchini—not mush. (To easily peel and ready tomatoes for cooking see peeling suggestion on page 99.)

Fried Green Tomatoes

Ever since I saw the movie "Fried Green Tomatoes" I have become addicted to this dish.

Un-ripened tomatoes (i.e. still green), sliced
1 egg, beaten with 1 tablespoon water
Instant-mashed potato flakes
2 tablespoons Butter
2 tablespoons olive oil

Dip slices of tomato in beaten egg mixture and then roll in mashed-potato flakes. Gently sauté (in a single layer) in butter and olive oil until golden brown, turning once. Drain on paper toweling and serve. Lightly season with salt and pepper to taste.

Secrets for Success:

One day I ran out of bread crumbs and decided to substitute potato flakes—I was delighted with the result and now use them for many breading situations!

Skillet Zucchini

Are zucchini over-running your garden—fry up a batch for a delightful side dish, or even for a vegetarian entrée, along with a nice salad, and muffins or bread.

Zucchini, peel left on and sliced (use larger zucchini)
1 egg, beaten with 1 tablespoon water
Instant-mashed potato flakes
2 tablespoons butter
2 tablespoons olive oil

Wash zucchini and pat dry. Slice. Dip slices in beaten egg mixture and then roll in potato flakes. Gently sauté (in single layer) in butter and oil, turning once. Sauté in batches and drain on paper toweling. Keep warm in low oven. Add more butter and oil, as/and if necessary, for each batch. Lightly season with salt and pepper and serve.

Secrets for Success:

The next time a neighbor offers you their extra zucchini, don't hesitate to accept.

Creamed Spinach

No spinach eaters in your family? Surprise them with this recipe.

2 pounds fresh spinach, washed, cooked, drained and chopped
   (or substitute 2 packages frozen-chopped spinach, cooked to
   package directions and drained)
2 to 3 tablespoons butter
1 green onion, minced fine
¼ cup fine bread crumbs
½ teaspoon salt
¼ teaspoon pepper
Dash of nutmeg
1 cup condensed cream of mushroom or cream of celery soup
Dabs of butter, at serving time
Parmesan cheese, at serving time

Heat butter in skillet on medium heat setting. Add bread crumbs, minced onion and seasonings, sautéing briefly till very lightly browned. Add in cooked and drained spinach, mixing well, to heat through. Stir in soup and heat through. Serve in individual cups on the side. Garnish each serving with a slight dab of butter and a sprinkling of Parmesan cheese.

Secrets for Success:
When draining spinach, be sure to squeeze out extra liquid.

Fried Eggplant

A great side dish on its own—or upgrade to **Parmigiana-Style.** *Estimate 1 to 2 slices per person for either recipe.*

1 egg plant, peeled and cut into ½ -inch thick (chop-size) slices
Salt
1 egg, beaten with 1 tablespoon of water or milk
Instant mashed potato flakes
Canola oil to cover bottom of skillet
1 to 2 tablespoons butter
Salt and pepper

Slice egg plant and sprinkle with salt. Let stand briefly. Pat off excess moisture with paper toweling. Dip egg plant in egg mixture, then coat with potato flakes. Slip slices into hot oil and butter. Do not crowd skillet. Fry until golden brown, turn and fry second sides. Lower heat if browning too quickly and continue to sauté gently until tender... Total cooking time approximately 10 to 15 minutes. Season with salt and pepper. Serve as is. Or top with your favorite warmed pasta sauce and a sprinkling of Parmesan cheese, to make **Eggplant Parmigiana-Style.**

Secrets for Success:
Don't crowd skillet when frying the eggplant and drain on paper toweling before serving.

Mom's Potato Patties

Economical, but oh so good, this is another of my favorite "comfort foods."

2 cups leftover, cooked mashed potatoes
1 egg yolk (or can use whole egg, depending on consistency of potatoes)
½ pie plate flour, or bread crumbs, seasoned with salt and pepper
2 tablespoons canola oil
2 tablespoons butter
Grated Parmesan cheese, optional

In a bowl, using a fork, mix leftover potatoes with yolk or egg, just until blended. With your hands, form about ½ - cupfuls into individual patties. (Patties will be delicate.) Gently dredge in the seasoned flour or breadcrumbs. Heat oil and butter in pan on a medium setting and gently place patties in skillet. Sauté until golden, turning once. Add more butter as/and if needed. Sprinkle with Parmesan cheese, turning and cooking just a minute more. (Do this for each side, being careful not to burn Parmesan. This can be an optional step—patties are good plain or with the Parmesan.) Lightly season with additional salt and pepper to taste. Serve with leftover meat and gravy, or as a side dish to a new meal.

Secrets for Success:
These potato patties will break apart very easily, so use a spatula for turning and removing from pan.

Aaron's Latkes (Potato Pancakes)

Yummy, yummy, yummy!

3 large potatoes, peeled
1 egg, beaten
1 to 2 tablespoons matzo meal
Dash of salt and pepper
Finely diced onion (optional)
Cooking oil
Applesauce, at serving time

Grate potatoes by hand on fine side of grater. Let grated potatoes drain in a sieve placed above a bowl—discarding the starchy liquid. (Potatoes will oxidize to a pink color, but that is okay.) Mix drained potatoes with egg, matzo meal, salt and pepper, and onion. Form into flat patties and fry in hot oil for about 4 to 5 minutes, turning once. Hold in warm oven, till all batches are fried. Serve warm with applesauce.

Secrets for Success:
Be sure to drain off starch when grating potatoes.

Old Fashioned Cottage Fries

This hearty dish is great served with scrambled eggs, for a "breakfast at dinner." Also great served with a lighter entrée, such as fish—bringing back memories of shore-cooked lunches, right in your kitchen.

Potatoes, washed and peeled (or leave peel on if you wish)
1 medium onion, chopped
Canola oil to cover bottom of skillet
1 tablespoon butter
Salt and pepper to taste

Cut potatoes in half lengthwise, then each half lengthwise into thirds—ending with 6 long slices per potato. Slice these, cross-wise, into small pieces. Heat oil and butter in skillet. Fry potatoes and onions until, soft, tender and caramelized brown, about 20 minutes. Turn down heat if browning too fast. Season with salt and pepper. Can also sprinkle with grated Parmesan toward end of cooking.

Secrets for Success:
Keep it simple. Let the caramelized onions flavor the dish, along with your seasonings of salt and pepper.

Leftover Fried Potatoes

*Home alone for a night? Have a leftover baked potato?
Cook this up for a quick, satisfying, economical dinner.
If you have several leftover potatoes, cook up a skillet-
full to go with grilled meats, or even eggs.*

Leftover cooked baked potatoes
Minced onion, to taste
Salt and pepper, to taste
Dash of paprika
Butter

Carefully slice cooked potatoes. Gently sauté potatoes
with minced onion and seasonings in butter, till lightly
browned, turning once in a while with a spatula. This
recipe will cook up quickly, since the potatoes are
already cooked. Can pass sour cream and chives for a
garnish if you wish.

Secrets for Success:
Sometimes the most simple can be the most satisfying...

Fried Apple Slices

The next time you are including sausages or bacon with your breakfast, cook up a batch of apple slices in the drippings to add an easy, yet "pizzazz-y" side dish to your meal.

Apples, peeled, cored, and cut into ½ -inch thick rings
Sugar (brown or white)
Pan drippings from breakfast sausages or bacon

After removing breakfast sausages or bacon from skillet, sauté sliced apples in the pan-drippings. While cooking, sprinkle with a little brown sugar to glaze. Turn with spatula, cooking both sides just until apple slices are warmed through and tender, but still hold their shape. Do not over cook. Serve warm along with the rest of your breakfast menu.

Secrets for Success:
Use tart cooking apples for best flavor.

Suzi's Buckwheat Kasha

Serves 4

Kasha can be served as a side dish, or can actually be served as a light entree, along with a nice salad and some rustic bread or muffins. A Middle Eastern and Russian staple, buckwheat just happens to be a complete source of protein, containing the essential amino acids plus iron and vitamin B. Suzi, my health-conscious cooking friend, says her family includes this recipe at both their traditional holiday gatherings and everyday meals.

1 box medium granule Kasha (use Wolff's® brand; this recipe
    calls for 1 cup of kasha kernels)
1 cup bowtie noodles, cooked and drained
2 cups chicken broth
2 tablespoons butter
¼ teaspoon salt
Dash of pepper
Dash paprika
1 egg (or just the white of an egg)
¼ cup minced onion or shallot (optional, depending on taste
    preference)
Non-stick cooking spray

Boil bowties until soft, drain and set aside. In a small pan bring broth, butter and seasonings to a boil. In a small bowl lightly beat egg (or egg white) with fork. Add kasha kernels and stir to coat in the beaten egg. Set aside. Sauté minced onion briefly in non-stick sprayed skillet to soften. Remove onion and set aside. Place egg-coated kasha in skillet on medium-high to high setting. Stir and cook for approximately 2 to 3 minutes, or until egg has dried on kasha and kernels have separated. Reduce heat setting in skillet to low. Add back sautéed onion to skillet. Add boiling broth mixture and bowties, stirring to mix all. Cover tightly and simmer for 7 to 10 minutes, or until kasha kernels are tender and liquid has been absorbed. Serve immediately. (Any meat gravy makes a nice addition when serving.)

Secrets for Success:

With a little adaptation this recipe can be turned into a substantially satisfying vegetarian dish.

Rodney's Fried Flowers

This dish is for all you gardeners out there. I have a friend who has a huge garden, and upon occasion fries up his zucchini blossoms for a special treat. Once in a while I come across these delectable squash blossoms in a specialty market, and when I do, I make his recipe.

Freshly picked, new zucchini blossoms, pistil and stamen
  removed
1 egg, beaten with a little milk
A pie plate of flower, seasoned with salt and pepper
Olive oil to a depth of ¼ to ½ -inch

Gently dip flowers in egg mixture, then roll in lightly seasoned flour to coat. Fry in hot olive oil till delicately golden and puffed a bit. Do not crowd pan. Drain on paper toweling. Eat immediately.

Secrets for Success:
Befriend someone who has a wealth of zucchini plants in their garden!

Rodney's Frittata for Two

Rodney also has a passel of chickens and access to freshly laid eggs.

5 eggs per omelet, beaten
Chopped onion, braised in olive oil
Chopped potato, braised in olive oil
Salt and pepper, to taste

Mix ingredients and pour into skillet, heated with olive oil. Cook on one side, stirring and adjusting egg mixture to get center done. Turn onto an oiled plate. Slide back into skillet to cook second side. Serve with the zucchini blossoms for a light summer dinner. Add a glass of chilled white wine or refreshing iced tea.

Secrets for Success:

An epicure, Rodney proves that men don't have to always eat "meat and potatoes" to have dinner be a success.

Bananas as a Vegetable

Tired of serving the same old veggie? Surprise your family (especially your children) with this side dish!

Variation # 1

Firm, under ripe bananas (nice and yellow, no brown spots)
Butter
Salt and pepper

Peel bananas and leave whole. Sauté in butter until golden brown on all sides, gently turning with a spatula. Bananas should be softened and tender when done, but still hold their shape. Very lightly season with salt and pepper. Serve warm in place of a vegetable. Make at least 1 banana per person.

Variation # 2

Sprinkle with 2 or 3 tablespoons of dark brown sugar as you are sautéing the bananas. Omit salt and pepper. Sauté until bananas are well glazed, but again don't over cook. You want the bananas to still hold their shape and be just warmed through and glazed. Serve warm. Can garnish with a dollop of sour cream if you wish to be fancy.

Secrets for Success:

The salty version or the sweet version, these are guaranteed to please adventuresome pallets. Great accompaniment to Mexican dinners.

Easy Apple Fritters

Fritters couldn't be easier, when you use a premixed pancake mix! This recipe is written to make a dozen fritters.

3 tart cooking apples, cored and sliced into thick rings
Fresh lemon juice
1 cup packaged pancake mix (the kind that you just add water to)
¾ cup water
Dash nutmeg
Dash cinnamon
Powdered sugar
Canola oil, at a depth of ½ -inch, heated to 360 degrees

Peel and core apples with an apple-corer. Cut each apple into 4 thick rings. Sprinkle with fresh lemon juice to prevent browning. Mix pancake mix, water and dash of nutmeg to make batter. Dip each apple slice into fritter-batter to coat. Slip into skillet of hot oil. Fry quickly, turning over to brown both sides. Cooking time approximately 5 to 6 minutes, or till golden brown and apples are tender. Do not crowd pan. Remove fritters with tongs and drain on paper toweling. Dust with powdered sugar. Serve warm.

Secrets for Success:

Do not crowd skillet when cooking. The key is to keep the oil consistently hot and circulating around each fritter for quick cooking and less oil absorption. Drain excess on paper toweling before serving.

Presentation—Plating, Consuming and Enjoying Your Meal

Visual presentation can be almost as important as taste for serving your meals successfully.

Plating meals rather than serving "family style" can be a great way to "portion control"—who eats what and how much. It can also be a nice tradition for the "head of the household" to serve up the portions, pausing for a moment to express gratitude for the bountiful food and appreciation for family before the meal is served.

Piling copious amounts of food on each plate can seem insurmountable and overwhelming, especially to a small child. The old saying "less is more" applies here, as we can always come back for seconds. And the application of the "one bite rule" or "try a bite, you might like it" may get a child to venture forth, accepting a newly found taste to his or her repertoire.

Getting in the habit of eating half of what's on your plate, and saving the rest for a snack or lunch later, is good way to regulate your food intake and literally "diet" without self-deprivation. Never force a person to eat more than they wish or more than they are hungry for.

Using color, texture, contrasts and compliments of foods, garnishes and embellishments, herbed seasonings instead of salt, and well-rounded meals can enhance the dining experience. Even one-pot dinners taste better with the compliment of a salad and muffins or bread. Attention to detail can make an ordinary meal extraordinary.

"Timing is all." When the meal is ready, **it's ready!** You've paid hard-earned money to buy and prepare your food. It is literally an investment that affords you one of life's most basic of pleasures. Eat it when it's ready—not a half hour later, when it has lost its peak flavor and consistency, or needs to be re-warmed.

Pause before dessert. A cup of coffee or hot tea can be an exquisite ending to a meal, settling the digestive tract. Save dessert for later.

Even if you live alone, plating your meal on a pretty plate, getting out a linen napkin and putting on some soft music can enhance your dining experience. Adding a special garnish, even if it is a tomato picked from your garden, a slice of summer melon, or a wedge of lemon in your ice water, pleasure can be added to your meal...

Chapter Five: "Beyond the Pan"

Twenty-two non-cook "side attractions" to assemble while your entrée is cooking

"Beyond the Pan" is a very special chapter—not devoted to skillet-cooked recipes, but to "non-cook" recipes that you can "assemble" while your entrée is cooking. Salads, Slaws, Salsas, and two "Soups" round out this chapter. Raise your dinner from "one-pot to full menu-ed" with these healthy selections.

"Beyond the Pan" Index

Rustic Broccoli and Grape Salad

A mélange of flavors and textures, this hearty salad is a hit every time.

1 large bunch fresh broccoli, cut into small bite-size pieces, using flowerets and tender portions of stalks
1 cup green seedless grapes, halved
1 cup diced celery
¼ cup raisins
1 bunch green onions, with tops, diced
1 (1 pound package) bacon, cooked crisp, drained and coarsely crumbled
1 package slivered almonds, sautéed in 1 tablespoon butter till very lightly browned. Cool.
1 cup mayonnaise
½ cup sugar
1 tablespoon vinegar

In a serving bowl mix first 7 ingredients together. Set aside. To make dressing mix mayonnaise with sugar and vinegar till well blended. Toss salad-mixture with mayonnaise-dressing mixture to blend well. Store covered in refrigerator until serving time. Can make salad a day ahead and refrigerate overnight.

Secrets for Success:
To reduce calories and fats in this recipe: toast almonds dry on baking sheet in 325-degree oven (eliminating the butter called for), use low-fat mayonnaise, and microwave the bacon. Eliminate the bacon altogether and you have a tasty yet hearty vegetarian salad.

Alvina's Orange and Onion Salad

When I moved into my little "antique" house on the shores of a sparkling lake, my girl friends threw a surprise house-warming party for me. Each recipe came presented in a bowl or dish for me to keep! This salad, presented in a beautiful wooden bowl, was one of those gifts.

¼ cup salad oil
1/3 cup vinegar
2 teaspoons salt
1/3 cup sugar
Mixed salad greens, washed, dried and kept chilled until serving
   time
Mandarin oranges, drained
Red onion, sliced into thin rings
Canned pineapple chunks, drained
Canned pitted black olives, drained
Jarred or canned artichoke hearts, drained

Make a basic vinaigrette dressing by shaking first 4 ingredients in a screw-top jar. Set aside at room temperature. Fill a salad bowl with greens and remaining fixings in order given. Store in refrigerator, covered with damp-paper toweling to keep chilled and fresh. At serving time re-shake the vinaigrette to blend well and lightly "dress" salad, tossing gently to mix. Serve immediately from a beautiful wooden salad bowl.

Secrets for Success:

Add pizzazz to your salad (as in this recipe) by combining colorful and unexpected ingredients. Be creative, add the attention of detail and raise your salad from ordinary and boring to tasty and spectacular. Always "dress" your salad just before serving.

Aunty Joan's Spinach Salad

Grapefruit sections and thin slivers of water chestnut add interest to this salad.

1 pound fresh spinach leaves
Water chestnuts, drained, dried and cut paper thin
Canned grapefruit sections, drained (Reserve liquid if making your own vinaigrette.)
Vinaigrette dressing, use store-bought (such as delicate Raspberry or Balsamic flavored) OR make the **Grapefruit Vinaigrette Recipe** on next page!
Bacon, cooked and crumbled, at serving time (see page 59 for conveniently micro-waved bacon)

Sort and wash fresh spinach leaves. Shake in colander and pat dry with paper towels. Trim any tough stems and veins from larger leaves. (By gently paring and pulling off the stems, the stringy-spinach veins will follow from the backs of the leaves.) This step is not necessary on smaller, tender leaves. Pre-assemble spinach in bowl. Top with the grapefruit sections and water chestnuts. Store un-dressed salad in refrigerator, covered with damp paper toweling until time of serving. Lightly pour on your favorite room-temperature bottled vinaigrette or use Joan's homemade Grapefruit Vinaigrette (see next page) and toss to coat all. Garnish with crumbled bacon and serve.

Grapefruit Vinaigrette

3 tablespoons reserved juice from the canned grapefruit
3 tablespoons white wine vinegar
1 tablespoon soy sauce
½ teaspoon sugar
½ teaspoon Dijon-style mustard
A pinch of salt
½ cup salad oil

Combine all and shake in a screw top jar to blend. If storing dressing be sure to re-shake at time of tossing salad. Use the dressing at room temperature.

Secrets for Success:

As with any salad, the secret is to prep and store the greens dry/damp and chilled, adding the dressing at the last minute. If using bottled dressing be sure to shake to blend well, just before using. Vinaigrettes shake-up and blend better when not coagulated and cold straight from the fridge, but rather at room temperature—so let dressing stand out on the counter for a while before gently coating and tossing the salad. If you've pre-made a homemade dressing be sure to re-shake it just before using.

"I'll take the Number 12 Salad"

Twelve ingredients add up to big taste in this salad. This recipe makes 6 servings.

½ head iceberg lettuce, coarsely shredded
½ head of romaine, torn
1 zucchini, thinly sliced, peeled or unpeeled—your choice
½ cup thinly sliced radishes
2 green onions, chopped with tops
2 tablespoons crumbled blue cheese
¼ cup olive oil
2 tablespoons dry red wine
1 tablespoon vinegar
½ teaspoon salt
¼ teaspoon dry mustard
¼ teaspoon paprika

In a screw-top jar shake and blend last 6 ingredients listed. Set aside at room temperature. Assemble first 6 ingredients in serving bowl. Cover with damp-paper toweling and chill until time of serving. Pour on dressing (shaking well again) and toss until greens glisten.

Secrets for Success:

Use the freshest produce to make your perfectly crisp salad. Toss with room-temperature dressing at the last minute.

Cauliflower Escabeche

Crispy, crunchy and colorful this recipe makes a decorative crudités-style vegetable salad for 6.

½ head cauliflower, chopped into bite-size pieces
1 green bell pepper, ribbed and seeded, rustically cut
1 red bell pepper, ribbed and seeded, rustically cut
1 yellow bell pepper, ribbed and seeded, rustically cut
1 can pitted black olives, drained
¼ cup olive oil
2 tablespoons white wine vinegar
½ teaspoon salt
Freshly cracked pepper
½ teaspoon chili powder
2 cloves garlic, smashed and minced very fine

Blend and shake last 6 ingredients in screw-top jar to make marinade. Set aside at room temperature. Arrange cauliflower, bell peppers and black olives in a glass bowl. Add the shaken marinade and mix to coat all. Cover and refrigerate until serving time. Toss all to coat again just before serving.

Secrets for Success:
The freshest and choicest produce possible is key for this pretty salad.

Pineapple Slaw

A nice twist on traditional coleslaw, this recipe makes 4 delightful servings.

2 cups finely sliced and chopped cabbage, or use a pre-packaged coleslaw-mix
1 cup canned pineapple chunks, drained (reserve juice)
½ cup raisins, softened in 2 tablespoons of reserved pineapple juice
2 tablespoons mayonnaise
2 tablespoons sour cream
Romaine lettuce leaves for serving
Paprika, optional

Toss cabbage-mix, drained pineapple and "plumped" raisins with mayonnaise and sour cream to combine well. Chill. Serve individual portions mounded on romaine lettuce leaves. Dust with paprika for color. Recipe may be doubled or ingredients altered to your liking.

Secrets for Success:
Soaking the raisins in a little pineapple juice reconstitutes them from dried and chewy, to plump and tender.

Cile's "Magic" Coleslaw

Newly-married, a novice-cook to say the least, my dear mother in law took me under her wing. This recipe is as old and as easy as they come! I can still remember the 'magic' as she showed me how the cream and vinegar automatically thickened...

Shredded cabbage
Shredded carrot
Cream (about ½ to ¾ cup)
Cider vinegar (about 1 to 2 tablespoons)
A little sugar
A smidge of salt and pepper
Individual lettuce leaves, at serving time
Paprika, at serving time

For convenience use a pre-packaged coleslaw-mix—or, like my mother in law, finely slice and chop your own. While dinner is cooking, in a small bowl stir cream together with a little cider vinegar till thickened. Add sugar, salt and pepper to taste. The dressing will automatically thicken as you stir. Pour dressing over cabbage/carrot mix and toss to coat all. Chill salad in fridge until serving time. Serve mounded on individual lettuce leaves. Dust with paprika for color.

Secrets for Success:

The secret to the automatic thickening process is the fat in the cream interacting with the 1 to 2 tablespoons of cider vinegar. You must use cream for this to work. Make the slaw once or twice and you'll know exactly the amounts to use for your particular taste.

Barbara's Best Seven Layer Salad

There's just something about seven layer salad; it's soooo good!—Not a new idea, but one that we should remember to use from time to time! There are many variations to the seven-layer-salad but I've adopted my friend's recipe as the one I like best.

Iceberg lettuce, torn or sliced
Celery, de-ribbed and sliced thinly on the diagonal
Green bell pepper, ribbed, seeded and diced
Red onion, diced or sliced thin
A layer of mayonnaise, spread over all (use low-fat)
A sprinkling of sugar
Shredded Cheddar cheese
Crumbled, cooked bacon (see page 59 for micro-waved bacon)

To assemble salad, first put torn or sliced lettuce in bottom of serving bowl, then top with layers of celery, then bell pepper, then onion. Next spread a layer of mayonnaise to cover. Sprinkle sugar over the mayonnaise. Top with shredded Cheddar cheese to cover, and lastly sprinkle on the crumbled bacon. Cover and refrigerate over night.

Secrets for Success:
Making this salad the night before or the morning of serving, gives the flavors a chance to meld—plus it is so convenient, to just pop it out of the fridge right at serving time.

Marily's Sweet Oil and Vinegar for Tossed Salad

This never-fail sweet oil and vinegar dressing was taught to me by a friend in college. Mix it up a batch at a time or keep it 'on tap' for spontaneous dinner salads.

1 shot glass sugar
1 shot glass salad oil of choice
1½ shot glasses vinegar of choice
Salt
Pepper
Paprika
Dry Mustard

In bottom of screw-top jar place the sugar. Add the oil. Pour on the vinegar. Shake in salt until it sinks in a ball. Crack in pepper to cover the surface. Then paprika to cover the surface. Then dry mustard to generously cover the surface. Cover jar and shake to blend well. Serve dressing at room temperature, tossed lightly with mixed-salad greens and fixings of choice.

Secrets for Success:

The no-fail formula for making this dressing is to add the ingredients in the order listed and to sprinkle in the salt just until it sinks in a ball. Use 1 to 2 tablespoons dressing per 1 to 2 cups of greens. There is nothing worse than a sodden or "overly dressed" tossed salad—greens should be lightly coated "just to glistening.

Mom's Easy-Pleasing Last Minute Side Salads

Need a quick salad?—Try one of these 'last minute' combinations to turn an everyday dinner into a well garnished meal:

#1
Canned peach halves, drained OR
  Canned pineapple slices, drained
Topped with Cottage cheese and a Maraschino cherry OR
  Cream cheese and a dusting of paprika
Lettuce leaves

Pick a fruit. Pick a garnish. Arrange each individual salad artfully on a lettuce leaf.

#2
Canned pear halves, drained OR
  Jarred spiced-apple rings, drained
Topped with mayonnaise and shredded Cheddar cheese
Lettuce leaves

Arrange pear half or 2 apple rings per salad on lettuce leaf and top with a dollop of mayonnaise and a sprinkling of shredded Cheddar cheese.

#3
Canned grapefruit sections, drained
Mandarin orange sections, drained
Russian salad dressing
Lettuce leaves

For each salad arrange several of both fruit sections on a lettuce leaf. Drizzle with Russian dressing.

#4
Jarred spiced peaches OR
  Jarred spiced, whole crab apples
Decorative kale leaves

Pick your fruit. Simply open the jar, drain, and place on a decorative kale leaf, right on the dinner plate.

#5
A platter of fresh, sugar-sweetened, tomato slices (see page 73).

#6
Lemon Sorbet or Sherbet

Serve in little side cups (in lieu of salads) to "refresh the palate and ease the taste buds" when eating spicy-hot meals.

Secrets for Success:
Grab a can or a jar from your well-stocked pantry, and a couple of staples from the fridge or freezer (just like our mothers used to do) and turn a simple meal into a well rounded dinner, with a last minute salad.

Green Goddess Salad

Bring this wonderful salad 'out of the recipe box' and back to your menu! I'm sure we all have a 'designer salad or two' just waiting to be re-discovered. So push away the everyday 'bottled-ranch' and branch out on your own!

1 cup mayonnaise (use low-fat)
4 to 6 anchovy fillets, mashed (yes…I know, but you need them for this recipe)
1 small green onion, including top, minced fine
2 tablespoons fresh parsley, minced fine
2 tablespoons fresh chives, minced fine
1 teaspoon dried tarragon leaves, crushed between fingers
1½ tablespoons tarragon or white-wine vinegar
Lettuce of choice
Pitted black olives, for garnish
Tomato wedges, for garnish

In blender, food processor or just a bowl, mix first 7 ingredients together to make a smooth dressing. Serve over lettuce of choice and garnish with black olives and tomato wedges.

Secrets for Success:

Why serve bottled dressing when you can make your own in minutes! Make your dressings one batch at a time for freshness and peak flavor at every meal. Throw out all those half-used bottles of commercial dressing that have been haunting your refrigerator! You'll be amazed at how wonderful, freshly-made can really taste—you'll never go commercial again!

Thousand Island Salads

Individual, crispy-cold iceberg lettuce wedges smothered with 1000 island dressing—Nothing delicate about this salad! This was my father's favorite.

1 cup mayonnaise (use low-fat)
¼ cup bottled-chili sauce
2 tablespoons finely chopped salad olives, including pimento
2 tablespoons finely minced green or red bell pepper
1 green onion, including top, minced
1 teaspoon Worcestershire
1 tablespoon sweet-pickle relish
1 tablespoon ketchup
Iceberg head lettuce, cut into wedges
Hard-boiled egg, finely chopped for garnish, optional

In a small bowl combine first 8 ingredients to make dressing. Cover and chill to meld flavors. Remove any outer, unattractive leaves from the head of lettuce. Slice into thick compact wedges and place on individual chilled salad plates. Spoon on dressing and garnish with finely chopped hard-boiled egg at serving time.

Secrets for Success:

Often underrated, this is one time iceberg lettuce is a must. Don't skimp on the salad dressing because this is a time when less does not equal more.

Bonus Recipe: This Thousand Island Dressing could be used as a dipping sauce for the shrimp recipes in chapter one (see pages 26 through 31 for shrimp recipes).

Cile's Blender-Blue Cheese Dressing for Salad

Why buy bottled—when you can make this so easily, just before dinner time.

1 (8 ounce) package cream cheese, softened
1 small package crumbled blue cheese
A dollop of mayonnaise
Salt to taste
Garlic powder to taste
Cream or milk, to arrive at desired consistency
Additional crumbles of blue cheese, for garnish
Fresh chives, for garnish
Freshly cracked pepper, for garnish

Using a blender, mix together softened cream cheese, blue cheese and mayonnaise. Season with a little salt and garlic powder to taste. Blending on high add just a little milk or cream to arrive at desired consistency. Dressing should be thick and creamy. Serve over salad greens of choice and garnish with additional crumbles of blue cheese, snipped chives and freshly cracked pepper.

Secrets for Success:

Blend dressing until ultra-creamy smooth and don't skimp on the blue cheese. If you don't have a blender, mix the dressing in a small bowl, using a dinner fork or a hand mixer.

The Art of Making a Salad

A word about matching lettuces and dressings:

For heavier creamy dressings and hearty oil and vinegars, select Iceberg, Romaine, raw spinach or sturdy-mixed greens.

For delicate vinaigrettes (such as Raspberry and Balsamic) try Bibb, Boston, Butter, garden varieties of leaf, and tender baby spinach, or mixed Spring greens.

When in doubt serve the versatile Romaine.

Reserve iceberg wedges for Thousand Island Dressing; and torn iceberg, mixed with other greens, for Creamy Blue Cheese.

Use vinaigrettes at room temperature, re-shaking to mix thoroughly just before dressing salad.

Dress salads just before serving.

"Design" your salad with your entrée in mind.

Use greens promptly after purchase. Wash them and pat dry. Store in dampened paper toweling, in non-air tight plastic bags, until ready to use.

To store mushrooms, loosen tightly wrapped saran around package—mushrooms need to breathe. Never wash mushrooms—clean by gently brushing.

No-Egg Caesar Salad

A sophisticated salad—this is an elegant choice when company is coming for dinner. Toss it at the table for extra flair and flavor. Some people like to add a 1-minute coddled egg to the dressing, but I elect not to.

4 to 6 anchovy filets, drained, broken and mashed (or 3 inches of anchovy paste)
1 garlic clove, smashed and minced very fine
1 to 2 tablespoons Dijon mustard
2 tablespoons white-wine or tarragon vinegar
2 tablespoons fresh lemon juice
A dash of Worcestershire sauce
9 tablespoons virgin olive oil
2 heads romaine lettuce, washed, dried, and torn or cut into pieces
Freshly cracked pepper
Croutons (see recipe page 248)
1 to 2 tablespoons capers, drained
Fresh Parmesan cheese, sliced into wafer-thin curls

In a small glass bowl smash anchovy filets (or use anchovy paste) and garlic to make a smooth paste. Stir in mustard, vinegar, lemon juice and Worcestershire sauce till blended. (The mustard will act as a binder in place of using a coddled egg.) While stirring with a wire whisk, slowly drizzle in olive oil blending all the while. Place torn romaine lettuce leaves in large salad bowl. Top with croutons and freshly cracked pepper. Drizzle on room-temperature dressing, tossing to coat until greens glisten and croutons have "picked up" some of the dressing. (Use a ratio of about 1 to 2 tablespoons of dressing per 1 to 2 cups of salad greens.) Sprinkle on capers (and additional anchovy filets if desired). Garnish salad with thin curls of fresh Parmesan cheese and serve immediately.

Secrets for Success:

Using anchovies is a must for the salty taste, traditional to authentic Caesar salad. Adding capers as a garnish is a nice touch. If you absolutely cannot stand anchovies, substitute all capers, and a little of the jarred caper juice, in their place. Mixing in a fine quality olive oil at a drizzle and all the while using a wire whisk, blends the dressing well before you lightly toss your salad. Salad should be dressed just at serving time so greens don't wilt. A potato peeler works very well for making paper-thin Parmesan cheese curls to garnish your salad. If you don't have fresh Parmesan, be sure to substitute a generous sprinkling of its grated counterpart.

Vegetarian variation: Replacing anchovy filets totally with capers can turn a Caesar Salad into a vegetarian salad, although the resultant taste won't be quite the same as the traditional-anchovy-version. (Capers are little salty buds from a plant grown in the Mediterranean. They look kind of like pickled peas. Although you can get them in gourmet sections to experience fresh... I highly recommend the more traditional brine-pickled kind in little jars. Like caviar, you might find them to be an acquired taste.)

Cranberry Relish

Bold and spicy, this little relish adds zip to your meal.
This recipe makes about 11/2 cups.

1 (8 ounce can) whole cranberry sauce
1 small onion, diced
¼ to ½ cup golden raisins
¼ cup walnuts, toasted and coarsely chopped
2 fresh lemon wedges, sliced very thin, peel left on
1 teaspoon Dijon-style mustard
½ teaspoon prepared horseradish
¼ teaspoon hot sauce

In a glass bowl, stir together cranberry sauce, minced onion, raisins and toasted nuts. Stir in the thinly sliced lemon pieces. Stir in mustard, horseradish, hot sauce and adjust to your taste. Cover and let stand (while your meal is cooking) to meld flavors. Pass as a side relish.

Secrets for Success:

To toast (a small amount of) nuts stir in a dry pan over medium heat 2 to 4 minutes, just to release oils and nuts become aromatic. Cool and chop. You can omit this toasting process if you wish, but it really does add to the taste and texture of the nuts used in this recipe—an easy detail to make your relish the best!

"Change of Pace" Salsa

This salsa? salad? relish? is exactly as it says—a refreshing 'change of pace' to serve beside your meal.

1 cup peeled and finely chopped fresh peach, or nectarine, or mango
1 cup finely chopped cucumber, which has been peeled and seeded
2 to 3 green onions (with tops), finely sliced
2 tablespoons snipped parsley
1 tablespoon sugar
1 tablespoon salad oil
1 tablespoon vinegar
1 teaspoon grated, fresh gingerroot

Place first 4 ingredients in a glass bowl. Shake sugar, oil, vinegar and gingerroot in a small-screw top jar till blended. Pour into bowl and toss all to mix. Store covered in refrigerator until serving time. Serve as a salsa or relish-accompaniment.

Secrets for Success:

Buy ripe fruit (at its peak) for optimum flavor in this recipe. Drained and chopped, canned freestone-peach halves can be substituted (in place of fresh) in a pinch...

Avocado Gazpacho Salad

This luscious recipe makes 6 individual salads.

3 perfectly ripe avocados
3 tablespoons fresh lemon juice
1½ cups peeled, seeded and chopped fresh tomato, drained of
    any excess juice
½ cup chopped zucchini or cucumber (your choice), dried on
    paper toweling
¼ cup chopped green bell pepper or green onion (your choice)
1 clove garlic, mashed and minced
2 tablespoons olive oil
1 tablespoon vinegar
½ teaspoon salt
1/8 teaspoon Tabasco® or similar hot sauce
Shredded lettuce
Sour cream
Snipped chives

Halve the avocadoes and carefully spoon out pulp into a glass bowl. Brush emptied avocado shells with fresh lemon juice, cover with plastic wrap, and chill in refrigerator until ready to use. Chop removed avocado pulp and gently toss with remaining ingredients (except shredded lettuce, sour cream and chives). Mound filling into the reserved avocado shells. Sprinkle a tiny bit of lemon juice over each salad, re-cover with plastic wrap and return to refrigerator until serving time. To serve, place each shell on an individual bed of shredded lettuce, on chilled salad plates. Top each serving with a dollop of sour cream and freshly snipped chives.

Secrets for Success:

Make this salad very near serving time and serve individually on chilled salad plates. When prepping the tomatoes and zucchini or cucumber, be sure to drain off any excess moisture and eliminate any seeds.

Vi's Vine Ripened Tomatoes with Mozzarella

The wonderful sun-ripened tastes of summer straight from her garden—Vi used to pick and prepare this salad right before dinner time.

Fresh, sun-ripened red garden tomatoes, cut into thick slices
Fresh mozzarella cheese, cut into slices
Olive oil (I like to use roasted-garlic flavored olive oil)
Balsamic vinegar
Fresh garden herbs, minced and crumbled

While dinner is cooking, slice the tomatoes and fresh mozzarella into equal size slices. Arrange alternately and overlapping slightly, in a single layer, on a platter. Drizzle with a good olive oil and a hint of balsamic vinegar. Garnish with freshly picked herbs of your choice. Serve at room temperature.

Secrets for Success:

Fresh and ripe are the keys to this simple salad. If you don't have a garden a farmer's market will do. If choosing tomatoes from your supermarket, look for the ripest ones. Just as the quality of the tomatoes is important, so is the fresh mozzarella--soft and smooth yet firm, it is a tremendous accent to the sun ripened tomatoes. —Four choice ingredients and some additional fresh herbs speak volumes in this simple dish.

Jellied Madrilène

Impressive—yes. Easy—yes. This sophisticated, little recipe is perhaps an acquired taste—but one that I remember my mother serving for very special occasions. I still love it today as a refreshing and unusual first course, before I bring dinner to the table. This recipe is written to make 6 first-course servings.

2 cans beef-jellied consommé, chilled in the can, in the
   refrigerator.
Sour cream
Chives

At time of serving mound the jellied consommé into chilled, fancy stemmed glasses. Top with a dollop of sour cream and snipped chives. Serve immediately as a first course.

Secrets for Success:

The colder the ingredients the better! —If you want to get really fancy, skip the chives and top the sour cream with a little caviar!

Gazpacho

I became 'addicted' to this cold soup while traveling in Spain. Each locale had their slightly different version. This recipe makes 4 servings and adds a wonderful first course to any meal. So skip the salad tonight and literally serve it in 'soup form'.

4 cups tomato juice (your choice of spiciness and brands)
3 tablespoons virgin olive oil
2 tablespoons wine vinegar
Cucumber, diced
Onion, diced
Tomato, seeded and chopped
Avocado, chopped
Salad croutons for garnish (*or toast your own)
Snipped chives
Lime wedges
Sour cream

Blend first 3 ingredients and chill. In chilled, shallow bowls (also called soup plates) place portions of diced cucumber, onion, tomato and avocado. Pour on the chilled "soup." Garnish with crisp croutons, snipped chives and more diced cucumber. Serve cold. Pass lime wedges and sour cream on the side.

Secrets for Success:

If you like a spicier soup, select a spicy-flavored tomato juice or add a cup of Bloody-Mary-Mix to the recipe.

*To toast your own croutons: simply cube day old bread and stir fry dry or with a dab of butter and some spices (your choice) in a hot pan. Or bake (dry) on a cookie sheet in low oven until crisped.

Spinach and Strawberry Salad

A surprising mix, strawberries and spinach make an unusual combination. The watercress adds a tangy flavor to this out-of-the-ordinary, colorful salad. This recipe makes 4 to 6 refreshing servings.

4 cups torn spinach, washed, de-veined and patted dry with paper toweling
1 cup watercress (or substitute 1 to 2 cups packaged mixed-spring greens)
1 cup sliced fresh strawberries
½ small red onion, sliced very thin
½ cup bottled balsamic or raspberry vinaigrette, room temperature

Arrange cleaned and dried greens in salad bowl. Top with sliced strawberries and sliced onion. Toss at time of serving with ½ cup balsamic or raspberry vinaigrette. Serve immediately on individual chilled salad plates.

Secrets for Success:

Chilled salad plates keep your salad fresher, brighter and crisper longer. Individual serving plates make a nice presentation. Using your dressing at room temperature makes for a lighter, more blended and more delicate tossing of the salad. Attention to detail can turn simple into spectacular...

Crazy Apple Salad

One day I overheard two women talking about "this fabulous salad" so I politely asked if I could have the recipe... I have served this salad on many occasions and every time I get asked to pass along the recipe!

3 Granny Smith apples, cored, chopped, peel left on
3 red delicious apples, cored, chopped, peel left on
1 bag of "Halloween-treat-size" Snickers® candy bars, chopped coarsely
1 carton Cool Whip®-style topping, thawed
1 cup mini marshmallows
Cashews (optional)

Chop apples and candy bars, and mix together in a bowl. Fold in the whipped topping and marshmallows. Store covered in refrigerator until serving time. At time of serving garnish the salad with cashews.

Secrets for Success:

Although the leftovers of this salad can be enjoyed the next day, it is best made fairly close to serving time and eaten that same day.

Chapter Six:
On the Sweeter Side
Skillet-cooked recipes to satisfy your "sweet tooth"

We have our entrees, we have our sides, we have our salads—now it's time for dessert. Finish off your meal with a delectable recipe from these skillet-prepared sweets. From Crepes to Rosettes, your electric skillet can help you prepare tantalizing desserts that will keep everyone coming back for more.

On the Sweeter Side Index

Orange Crème Sauce

Cousin to the rich sabayon sauce, this subtle and sublime sauce makes a delicate topping or filling, in place of traditional whipped cream. This sauce is excellent with crêpes, goes well with strawberries, and would be an excellent addition to Bistro Pound Cake (see page 271).

1/2 cup sugar
1 orange, juice and grated rind
2 egg yolks, beaten
1 cup heavy cream, whipped

Mix sugar with orange's rind and juice in a* double boiler. Cook until sugar dissolves. Add egg yolks and cook until mixture thickens, stirring constantly (I use a wire whisk). Chill. Whip cream and gently fold into chilled sauce, just before serving. Use as a delicate accent for many of the desserts that follow in this chapter. Keep sauce refrigerated.

Secrets for Success:

In a pinch I have used my electric skillet like a double boiler. Simmer water in the skillet. Place a bowl in the simmering "water bath" and proceed as if you are using a double boiler, gently heating and mixing the mixture in the bowl.

Crêpes:

Crêpes (French Pancakes) are delicate and tender, and (with a little practice) so easy to make. Their versatility can be used for so many dessert combinations. They can be made in advance, reserved, and finally assembled at serving time—adding sauces and fillings to make wonderful dessert combinations, some served warm and others cold.

Basic Crêpe Batter

1 cup flour
¼ teaspoon salt
3 eggs, beaten well
1¼ cups milk
2 tablespoons butter, melted

Mix together flour and salt. Set aside. Combine beaten eggs with milk and add to flour. Beat until batter is very smooth, with no lumps. Beat in melted butter. You now have your basic batter.

Dessert Crêpe Batter

To the basic batter above add:
2 tablespoons powdered sugar
2 tablespoons liquor, optional (such as Grand Marnier, Brandy or Rum)

For dessert crêpes add the powdered sugar to the basic flour/salt mixture. Add the optional liquor when you add the melted butter. This will make a sweet batter for dessert-style crepes. If you don't want to use liquor, you could experiment with adding just a little flavoring-extract (such as vanilla, almond, maple, etc. if you wish).

Cooking the Crêpes

Melt butter into a medium-hot skillet until foamy. Make crêpes, one at a time, by pouring a scant ¼ cup of batter into the skillet each time. Spread batter as thin as possible. Cook quickly until bottom side is gently browned and pancake is set (about 1 minute). Turn crêpe and gently brown second side (about 1 minute more). Remove and place on a sheet of waxed paper. Proceed with another crêpe, melting in more butter as necessary. When crêpes are cool, stack them between the layers of waxed paper. Wrap the stack and store in refrigerator. Crêpes may be made in advance, wrapped and stored in refrigerator for up to 5 days, or in the freezer (air-tightly wrapped) for a month.

Secrets for Success:

Blend batter until very smooth and literally the consistency of heavy cream. Crêpes must be cooked quickly in hot (but not burning) butter. Cool each crêpe and stack between waxed paper until ready to use—may be made ahead and stored in fridge 1 to 2 days.

Paul's Crêpes Suzettes

This was my father's favorite dessert when company came for dinner. He was famous for his Crêpes Suzettes and his ceremonious way of serving them. Betty would make a fabulous dinner and Paul would follow with his flaming dessert...

A batch of dessert crêpes, cooked and reserved for serving time (see previous page for dessert-batter recipe and instructions for cooking and storing)
½ stick butter, melted
½ cup freshly squeezed juice from fresh oranges
2 tablespoons sugar
¼ teaspoon zest from the orange peel
1 to 2 tablespoons Grand Marnier (optional), in a long handled ladle

Dad would make his pancakes in the afternoon and set aside. To make sauce, on a medium heat setting, melt butter in skillet. Add orange juice, sugar and zest. Stir and simmer till all is melted and combined. Place crêpes into sauce one at a time. Using tongs turn to coat both sides and fold in half. With your tongs fold the crêpe in half again, turning it over in the sauce one more time. Arrange the completely folded and coated crêpe to side of skillet. Proceed in the same manner with another crêpe. After all the crêpes have been arranged in the sauce, gently simmer just till heated through. Carefully ladle on the Grand Marnier and ignite. Flambé mixture till flame dies down. Serve warm, 2 or 3 per person, on warmed dessert plates, with remaining sauce spooned over each serving.

Secrets for Success:

Make your pancakes well ahead of time and reserve, so you are not flustered or rushed at dessert time. For the sauce, measurements are not really critical; you may adjust juice, butter and sugar to your personal liking. The use of a liquor is purely optional. (I myself like my crêpes "a l'orange style" without the liquor.) The sauce-recipe may be doubled or tripled for as much as you need to amply glaze and coat the amount of pancakes you are serving.

Crêpes a la Jubilee

Cherries Jubilee, rich vanilla ice cream—a favorite in our family and even more delicious when served over crêpes!

A batch of dessert crêpes, cooked and reserved (per instructions on pages 256-57)
1 can pitted dark sweet cherries, with juice
1 teaspoon cornstarch
2 tablespoons water
2 tablespoons sugar
¼ cup Brandy, in a long handled ladle
Vanilla ice cream at serving time

Set your skillet on a low setting. Heat the cherries with their juice until simmering. Mix cornstarch with water until smooth. Add cornstarch mixture to simmering cherries and stir until sauce is smooth and slightly thickened. Fold crêpes in half and in half again, arranging one by one into the sauce, turning with tongs to evenly coat. When all crêpes have been arranged in pan and heated through, sprinkle with a little sugar. Carefully pour on Brandy, ignite and flambé until flame dies down. Serve immediately. Serve 2 to 3 crêpes per person, on warm dessert plates with sauce and cherries spooned over each serving. Top with a scoop of rich vanilla ice cream.

Secrets for Success:

When flambéing any dish NEVER, never pour the liquor straight from the bottle. Some people prefer to warm and flambé the liquor right in the long-handled ladle, and then slide it, while flaming, into the dish. Another technique is to ladle the liquor onto the dish and then light the surface with a long-stick match or fireplace lighter. Anyway, a bit of caution should be taken—you're not trying to burn the house down, or singe your eye brows—you are just 'flavoring' the dish.

Crêpes Cardinal

Raspberries and strawberries—they were made for each other.

A batch of dessert crêpes, cooked and reserved (per instructions on pages 256-57)
1 package frozen raspberries, thawed
2 tablespoons lemon juice
2 tablespoons sugar
2 tablespoons Grand Marnier, optional
Whipped cream
Fresh strawberries, washed, sliced and sprinkled with sugar if desired

Make your crêpes in advance, cool and reserve until dessert time. To make sauce, thaw the package of raspberries and press the mixture through a sieve to remove seeds. Mix in lemon juice, sugar and optional liquor. Set aside. Whip heavy cream until stiff. Set aside. Slice strawberries and mix with a little sugar if desired. Set aside. To assemble, fold each crêpe around a filling of whipped cream. Top with sliced strawberries. Drizzle raspberry sauce over all. Top with a little more whipped cream. Serve immediately.

Secrets for Success:
Make everything ahead, keep chilled, and assemble at serving time.

Crêpes Cancun

Citrus-y yet creamy, tart but sweet, warm yet chilled, rich yet refreshing...

A batch of dessert crêpes, cooked and reserved (per
   instructions on pages 256-57)
2 tablespoons butter
2 tablespoons sugar
The juice from a lemon
The juice from an orange
Sweet cream
1 tablespoon Brandy
Rich vanilla ice cream, slightly softened
Sliced banana for garnish

On low-heat setting melt the butter and add the sugar. Squeeze in the juices from a lemon and an orange. Heat and stir to blend. Add a little sweet cream, stirring all to make a sauce. Add the brandy, stirring till all is heated through. Do not boil. Roll each crêpe (that you have made and reserved) around a filling of rich vanilla ice cream. Spoon warm sauce over each filled crêpe. Garnish with sliced banana. Serve immediately.

Secrets for Success:

Enjoy the contrast of the warm sauce over the ice cream-filled crêpes. Assemble right at serving time.

Kay's Strawberry-Crêpe Blintzes

Strawberries 'n cream—a match made in heaven.

A batch of dessert crêpes, cooked and reserved (per
   instructions on pages 256-57)
16 ounces cream cheese, softened
½ cup margarine, softened
½ cup powdered sugar
2 tablespoons milk
2 tablespoons Sherry
1 teaspoon vanilla extract
2 (10 ounce) packages frozen strawberries, thawed
2 tablespoons cornstarch
¼ cup water
Fresh strawberries for garnish

Make crêpes ahead of time and reserve. To make filling,
cream next 6 ingredients together until fluffy and reserve.
To make sauce simmer last 3 ingredients together until
thickened. Roll crêpes around about 3 tablespoons of
filling per crêpe and drizzle with warm sauce. Garnish
each serving with a fresh strawberry. Serve immediately.

Secrets for Success:

If you don't want to make your own sauce, buy a jarred
strawberry sauce and fold in a tablespoon of Sherry
and/or tablespoon of lemon juice to make it "seem
homemade." Serve sauce room temperature or warmed
(in the microwave).

Chocolate Crêpes

A chocolate lover's delight—indulgent, indulgent, indulgent...This recipe is for my daughter!

A batch of dessert-crêpe batter (see pages 256-57) to which
    you have added ¼ cup cocoa powder. Cook, cool and reserve
    between layers of waxed paper.
Chocolate ice cream, toffee-chocolate chip ice cream, coffee ice
    cream, vanilla ice cream, or any ice cream that you find
    compatible with chocolate
Jarred chocolate sauce
Whipped cream or whipped topping
Shaved chocolate curls or crumbled Heath® or Skor® bar

Make chocolate crêpes by sifting ¼ cup cocoa powder into the flower-sugar-salt portion of the dessert-batter recipe found on page 254. Proceed with continuing directions found on page 255, cooking crêpes and setting aside. When ready to serve, roll each chocolate crêpe around an ice cream filling of your choice (I like to use coffee ice cream) and arrange on dessert plates. Drizzle with chocolate sauce. Pile on some whipped cream or whipped topping. Garnish with shaved chocolate curls or crushed chocolate candy bar.

Secrets for Success:

To make chocolate curls, shave the chocolate off of a Hershey® chocolate bar, using a potato peeler. To crumble candy bars, put chilled candy bar in plastic bag and crush with a hammer, mallet or rolling pin.

Pumpkin Puff Pancakes

Puffy...filled with the taste of autumn...this recipe makes a great little addition to your 'pancake repertoire'.

1 cup flour
1 tablespoon sugar
2 teaspoons baking powder
½ teaspoon salt
½ teaspoon cinnamon
¼ teaspoon nutmeg
1 cup milk
½ cup canned, cooked pumpkin
2 eggs, beaten
2 tablespoons butter, melted
Cooking oil or spray

Mix dry ingredients together. Mix wet ingredients into dry mixture one at a time, in order given, to make a smooth batter. Using your skillet like a hot griddle drop batter by spoonfuls into greased skillet. Sauté pancakes (several at a time) till puffed and golden on both sides. As you make them, store on warm platter in 200-degree oven. Serve with butter and maple syrup.

Secrets for Success:
Buttermilk may be substituted in the batter for an old-fashioned treat.

Swedish Pancakes

Don't miss this special recipe of tender pancakes topped with applesauce—Backtrack to pages 124-125, chapter two, for the recipe.

Secrets for Success:

Bonus Recipe: Many variations can be added to Swedish Pancakes. Instead of the applesauce, used on pages 124-25, fruit syrups are delightful substitutes— especially Blueberry Syrup or the traditional Lingenberry Syrup, preceded by a dusting of powdered sugar. And of course, pure Wisconsin Maple Syrup (please use the real thing) is delicious too. Any way you eat them, Swedish Pancakes are a wonderful treat!

Grandmother's Prussian Pancakes

My mother's family came from Prussia...and this recipe immigrated to this country with her mother.

1 cup flour
½ teaspoon salt
1 cup whole milk
3 eggs, beaten well
Butter, lard or non-stick cooking spray to grease skillet
Jelly or Jam or Preserves
Powdered sugar
Crème Fraiche or sour cream, for garnish at serving time

Mix first 4 ingredients, in order given, to make a smooth batter. On medium-heat setting, using butter, lard, or non-stick spray to lightly grease heated skillet, brown each pancake, turning once. As second side browns, spread cooked-side of pancake with jelly or jam or preserves of choice. Roll up jelly-roll fashion and remove to plate. Serve warm, sprinkled with powdered sugar and garnished with crème fraiche, see recipes on next page, (or you can substitute everyday sour cream).

Secrets for Success:

Currant jelly, tart but sweet, makes a great choice for the rolled-up filling. And "souring your own cream" adds further authenticity to the dish.

Crème Fraiche

1 cup heavy (whipping) cream, room temperature
2 tablespoons buttermilk or yogurt, room temperature

Shake both ingredients together in a sterilized, covered jar. Let stand at room temperature, on an undisturbed counter top, all day or over night. Once crème fraiche has "proofed" it can be stored in fridge for up to 1 week. Use in place of sour cream.

Buttermilk-
Lemon Crème Fraiche

1 cup buttermilk
2 tablespoons juice from a lemon

Combine in small glass bowl or jar, cover and let stand (undisturbed) overnight at room temperature to thicken. Can use in place of sour cream. Recipe keeps for up to 1 week in refrigerator.

Aunty Joan's Russian-Style Pancakes

As a side note, Grandmother's versatile batter (page 266) can also be used for the following recipe. My sister often made this Russian-style variation for special occasions—although not a dessert, I include the recipe here because it is so special.

A batch of Grandmother's Prussian Pancake Batter, (use only the batter portion of recipe found on page 266)
Butter for cooking
Crème fraiche
Caviar

Using batter from Grandmother's recipe, cook pancakes in buttered skillet and stack on top of each other, keeping warm in low oven. To serve, cut stack into wedges (as if you are cutting a cake). Top each wedge with a dollop of crème fraiche (or thick sour cream). Add a generous dab of caviar to crown each serving. Serve as a special first course for an elegant brunch or dinner party, accompanied with a glass of champagne (optional).

Secrets for Success:
Elegant, rich, out of the ordinary...automatic success! For true authenticity, you could serve icy chilled vodka in place of the champagne.

Mother's Resourceful Pancakes

When it comes to "comfort food" these pancakes are another "biggy" for me. Devised through ingenuity and out of necessity (my mother kept a household through the Great Depression and two World Wars) her sturdy pancake recipe has stood the test of time and has actually become a Sunday morning favorite within our family. Even today...although we no longer have the need to skimp on ingredients...we have all become "addicted" to these one-egg pancakes.

1 full cup flour
1 full cup milk
1 "hollow palm" of salt (that's a lot of salt but don't be shy)
1 egg
Butter for cooking

Mix the 4 ingredients to make a smooth batter. Cook in buttered skillet, spreading batter to make 1/8 –inch thick pancakes. Sprinkle with sugar or cinnamon-sugar and roll up jelly roll fashion. Eat immediately. These are also excellent spread with maple syrup, folded in half and topped with a little more syrup.

Secrets for Success:
Do not expect tender, rich, egg-y, crêpe-y pancakes. These turn out rather chewy, or shall I say 'al dente'...but they are oh so good.

French Toast

French toast can be taken beyond white bread and maple syrup. Be inventive—try raisin bread (my favorite), sliced muffins, whole wheat bread, French bread, sliced croissants, Holiday stolen (another of my favorites), and even "Texas-toast-cut." Experiment with toppings such as preserves, fruit sauces, fresh strawberries and whipped cream, sugar and cinnamon, berry-flavored syrups, apple butter—the possibilities are many!

Sliced, day-old bread, or bread of choice
2 eggs, beaten with 2 tablespoons milk
Melted butter in skillet

Dip day-old slices of bread in egg mixture and slide into skillet. Sauté gently in melted butter, till lightly browned. Turn and sauté second side. Use a moderate heat setting so you don't burn butter or scorch toast. Serve warm, traditionally topped with maple syrup, or dusted with powdered sugar, or sprinkled with sugar and cinnamon—or invent your own topping!

Secrets for Success:
Cook gently and slowly, so egg-coating doesn't become tough and rubbery. A minor detail like this can elevate your French toast to delicate and sublime.

"Bistro" Pound Cake

Rich and elegant, this dessert approaches the level of sinful.

6 (¾-inch) slices of store bought pound cake
2 eggs
4 tablespoons whole milk, or cream
Butter to coat bottom of skillet
Strawberry sauce or preserves, or fruit preserves of choice
 (such as apricot or cherry) at room temperature
Sour cream, whipped cream, or crème fraiche

Beat egg and milk, or cream, together to blend. As if you were making "French toast," dip pound cake slices in egg mixture to coat. Gently sauté in heated butter till golden brown, turning once. Serve warm, topped with strawberry sauce or your favorite fruit preserves. Garnish with whipped cream, sour cream, or crème fraiche. Accompany with full-bodied, after-dinner coffee or espresso.

Secrets for Success:
Gently sauté on moderate heat setting, so egg-coating doesn't toughen and become rubbery.

Rosettes

This recipe is a favorite of mine at holiday time, and I always get rave reviews when I serve these melt-in-your-mouth cookies. You must have an old-fashioned "rosette-iron" to accomplish this recipe. I inherited mine from my mother-in-law, but you can find rosette-irons in old-fashioned hardware stores or gourmet-specialty shops. They usually come as a boxed set, with a shaft and a selection of 4 interchangeable shapes (mimicking snow flakes).

2 eggs, slightly beaten
1 tablespoon sugar
¼ teaspoon salt
1 cup flour
1 cup milk
¼ teaspoon vanilla
Canola oil, about ½ -inch deep, heated to 365 degrees
Powdered sugar

To make batter, slightly beat the eggs. Beat in sugar and salt. Add flour and milk alternately, beating until batter is smooth. Bring oil up to temperature in electric skillet. (Theoretically you need a deep fryer for these, but I have carefully used my electric skillet with the same success.) Place Rosette iron in skillet to heat in the oil. Dip heated iron into batter to cover sides. Do not let batter run over onto the top. Immerse battered iron completely in oil and brown for 25 to 30 seconds. Cookie should flare off the iron and slip into the oil, or can be easily removed from the iron once cooked and crisp. Drain each cookie on paper toweling as they are done. Re-submerge iron in hot oil before dipping into batter for next cookie. When finished with cookies, dust with powdered sugar pressed through a sieve. Rosettes are very delicate and are best if eaten same day or next day. (However they can be stored, once cooled, in an airtight tin for 5 days.)

Secrets for Success:

Be sure to be extremely careful when using a skillet filled with hot oil. Make sure it is firmly placed on a stable counter-surface. And make sure the cord is tucked away—not fully extended, for someone to trip on, or get caught in! Make sure the skillet is out of reach of small children and pets, or someone dashing to answer the phone! I know I sound like I'm lecturing—but "safety knows no season" as a friend of mine once said.

So please regard my cautious warning, for any and all of these recipes! Be sure to turn- off and un-plug your skillet, whenever you are done with a recipe! And be sure to use your appliance safely and respectfully.

Easy Pleasing Donuts

Quick and fun—they are almost as good as the real McCoy!

A tube of refrigerated biscuits or buttermilk biscuits
Hot Canola oil, to a depth of ¼ to ½ -inch

Separate biscuits and lay on waxed paper. Using the top of a pop bottle as a cookie cutter, punch out a "donut hole" from the center of each biscuit. Fry the biscuits (and the holes) in 375 –degree oil, turning over to get both sides. Fry "donuts" just a minute or two on each side, or until deep-golden brown. Cooking shouldn't take longer than 5 to 6 minutes. Holes should take less time. Remove with tongs and drain on paper towels before serving. Sprinkle with cinnamon-sugar or powdered sugar. Or, frost with icing and sprinkle with Jimmies.

Secrets for Success:
Oil must be at a temperature of 375 degrees for best results. Do not crowd pan. Be extremely careful when using hot oil!

Mother's Old Fashioned Apples 'n Cream

A classic for an autumn or winter "comfort food"... simmered-to-perfection apples, with the taste of caramelized sugar and a hint of cinnamon. Nuts and/or raisins can be added too, if you wish.

1 apple per person
1 teaspoon butter per apple
1 teaspoon brown sugar per apple
1 dash of cinnamon per apple
Water, to cover bottom of skillet
Half-and-Half cream, at serving time

Choose good apples suitable for cooking. Wash and core. Pare off a strip of peel around the top of each apple (about 1/3 way down apple). Place in skillet. Fill each apple center with butter, brown sugar and cinnamon. Add a little water, around the filled apples, to cover bottom of skillet. Put on cover. Start with a high-heat setting to bring apples and water up to simmer. Once simmering, reduce to low-medium setting and simmer the apples until tender, but they still hold their shape— about 30 minutes, basting occasionally with skillet juices if you wish. Add more water as/and if necessary while cooking the apples. Carefully remove apples from skillet and serve warm in individual dessert dishes. Pass (luxurious) half-and-half cream to pour over apples.

Secrets for Success:
Half-and-Half cream just makes this dessert ever so rich and satisfying!

Fruit Fritters

"Fritter away your time" with this versatile recipe...

1 cup flour
1 teaspoon baking powder
Dash salt
2 tablespoons sugar
1 egg, beaten
1/3 cup milk
1 tablespoon butter. melted
1 cup canned, crushed pineapple, well drained
  OR 1 cup drained fruit cocktail, chopped
Canola oil, for "deep frying"
Powdered sugar, for dusting.

Combine first four ingredients in a mixing bowl. In a separate bowl combine the egg, milk and melted butter. Stir wet mixture into dry mixture and blend batter until smooth. Stir in selected fruit. Do not overwork batter. Heat ¼ to ½ -inch Canola oil to a temperature of 350 degrees. Carefully drop batter by teaspoons-full into hot oil. "Deep fry" for about 5 minutes, turning once, or until golden brown. Remove with tongs and drain on paper towels before serving. Dust with powdered sugar. Serve in a towel lined basket to have as a breakfast treat with strong coffee or at "tea time." Or, serve as a side dish option with any meal.

Secrets for Success:

Again "safety knows no season"—be careful when using hot oil. You can make fritters ahead, drain on paper towels and hold in warm oven until dinner is ready. Try experimenting with other fruits, such as diced peaches or maraschino cherries.

Apple Fritters

Backtrack to page 217, chapter four, for this recipe

Bananas Foster

A wow of a dish...and so easy!

6 tablespoons butter
6 tablespoons brown sugar
6 firm but ripe bananas, peeled and cut into 3 or 4 slices, on the
  diagonal
½ cup rum (or substitute pineapple juice if you don't want to use
  a liquor; or use a mixture of the two—flavoring with just
  enough rum to taste)
½ teaspoon freshly grated orange zest (optional)
Vanilla ice cream, at serving time
Thin orange slices, twisted and placed on top as a garnish
  (optional)

Melt butter and brown sugar (using 1 tablespoon each
per banana) in medium-hot skillet to form a glaze. Add
the bananas and sauté just a couple of minutes to soften
just a little bit, turning to glaze all sides. Reduce heat
setting to low-simmer. Add the rum by using a long-
handled ladle and flambé till flames die down.
(Remember NEVER, never add liquors to a hot skillet,
straight from the bottle...unless you want to burn your
house down...and then no one will get to enjoy dessert!)
Stir in the orange zest. Serve bananas with sauce, warm,
over rich vanilla ice cream, in your fanciest dessert
dishes. Garnish each dessert with a delicate twist of
orange.

Pineapple Foster

Juicy Pineapple, rum, pound cake...hmmm, hmmm, hmmm.

Slices of fresh, ripe pineapple (or use canned rings, well
 drained)
Thin slices of pound cake
Whipped cream
Grated coconut or crumbled macaroon, for garnish

Sauté and flambé pineapple slices as in Banana Foster
recipe, cooking fresh pineapple until tender. Place a slice
of pound cake on each dessert plate. Drizzle with a tiny
bit of rum (optional). Top with warm pineapple and
sauce. Garnish with whipped cream. Sprinkle with a bit
of fresh coconut or macaroon.

Secrets for Success:

Do not overcook the fruit for either dessert—you want
the bananas or pineapple to retain their shape and just
be tender—not mushy. Use a spatula to gently turn and
remove the fruit.

Peach Melba

This recipe is dedicated my sister, Joan...what a wonderful cook she was!

1 peach half per person (use fresh [skinned] when in season),
   or canned, drained—both are delicious
1 tablespoon butter or non-stick cooking spray
1 package frozen raspberries, thawed, pureed in blender, then
   pressed through a sieve to remove seeds
2 teaspoons fresh lemon juice
2 tablespoons sugar
2 tablespoons Grand Marnier (optional)
Vanilla ice cream, at serving time

On low heat setting, melt butter in skillet. Add prepared raspberries, lemon juice and sugar, blending on simmer setting. Add peaches and continue to cook until glazed, warmed through, and tender. Turn off heat and add a splash of Grand Marnier. Place a peach half in each dessert dish. Top with a scoop of vanilla ice cream. Distribute sauce equally between servings. Serve immediately.

Secrets for Success:

If your fresh peaches aren't quite ripe enough to your liking, poach them in a little water or wine to soften. Then chill and proceed with recipe as written.

The sauce portion of this recipe, minus the peaches and butter, makes what is called **"Sauce Cardinal."** When she wasn't making Peach Melba, my sister served this sauce (cold) over fresh Strawberries with Pound Cake, or as a refreshing sauce over Lemon Sherbet—just another example of how flexible a recipe can be!! Sauce Cardinal can be made ahead and stored in the refrigerator for up to 4 days.

Aunty Joan's Sauce Cardinal

1 tablespoon butter or non-stick cooking spray
1 package frozen raspberries, thawed, pureed in blender, then pressed through a sieve to remove seeds
2 teaspoons fresh lemon juice
2 tablespoons sugar
2 tablespoons Grand Marnier (optional)

On low heat setting, melt butter in skillet. Add prepared raspberries, lemon juice and sugar, blending on simmer setting. Add a dash of Grand Marnier. Serve warm or cold over assorted desserts.

Recipe Index
(Recipes alphabetically listed under featured ingredient)

Eggs

Cheese

Chicken

Condiments, Relishes and Garnishes

Desserts (See Listing for Sweets)

Dumplings

Gravies, Pan

Sandwiches

Sausage Dishes

Sauces, -Pan

Turkey

Veal

Vegetables

Chapter Indexes
(Chronological list on beginning page of each chapter for quick and easy reference)

"Secrets for Success" Index
(Tips, Tricks and Miscellaneous information found throughout text)

Temperature Chart and Cooking-Method Guide

Most recipes require several different temperature-stages of cooking. Start by bringing your skillet and oil up to temperature. Add foods in order called for in recipe and begin by cooking on highest temperature called for. Reduce heat-settings "as you go" until the dish is done. You may have to remove and hold certain foods while raising heat-setting again to "finish" the dish (i.e. sauces and gravies and glazes) and then return held food back to skillet before serving.

Secrets for Success:

Get to "know" your electric skillet— temperatures used and times suggested for each cooking-stage will vary—according to amounts and thicknesses of ingredients in relation to the size of the skillet—to your personal preferences—and to brand names used. Different appliances will very in performance and dial-settings. Your appliance should come with general instructions and a brand name-guideline book to help you. Often, electric-skillet manufacturers include or offer a cookbook applicable for your designated purchase. Basically, anything that can be cooked in a pan can be cooked in an electric-skillet (or electric fry pan), and vice versa. With some experimentation and repetition you will become well-versed in how your pan works—no longer needing a temperature chart to guide you.

Dial-Settings	Cooking Method
0 to 200	Holding food when done
(Warm)	Holding food on a buffet table
220 to 270 (Low settings)	Covered simmering, stewing, braising and extended cooking.
(Low to Low-Medium) 220-300	Slow-cooking, covered, to avoid evaporation and to tenderize meats and vegetables (after initial browning at higher heat)
300 to 325 (Medium)	Grilling and griddle-style cooking
325 to 350	Sautéing, usually with butter
(Medium to High)	Gentle frying and browning for vegetables, potatoes and garlic
350-360 (High)	More aggressive frying, usually used to initially brown meats— followed by further cooking at lower temperatures while covered. At end of cooking, turn back up to medium-high to reduce and deglaze skillet juices to make gravy by continually stirring, thickening and condensing flavors to finish dish
360 to 375	Quick browning for meats
(High)	Searing, to lock in flavors; Quick Stir-frying (Heat setting may then be reduced to finish cooking.)
375 to 400	Shallow Pan Method for Deep-oil Frying
(Very High)	"French Frying" in deep oil; Very-quick sautéing, with a watchful eye—do not leave skillet untended. Oil must be very hot, so batters and breading do not absorb oil. Can reduce to 350 to finish.
425 (Highest)	Very hot setting to keep oil at 400 degrees for deep-frying when food is added to skillet, keeping oil temperature from dropping. Not all electric skillets have this setting.

Glossary of Many of the Cooking Terms Used in This Book

"Al dente"—An Italian term for cooking pasta just until tender but still slightly
  chewy, not over cooked, mushy, or soft

"Al fresco"—Dining out side, in the fresh air

Amandine—To serve with a garnish of sautéed butter and almonds

Baste—Spoon or brush liquids, melted butter, marinades and/or pan juices over an item while it's cooking, such as basting turkey or chicken to get a richly browned surface

Blanch—A quick plunging of food into boiling water for about 30 to no more than 60 seconds and then into ice water to stop the cooking process. Blanching tomatoes and peaches makes for easy removal of skins, without cooking the interior of the item.

Boil—Bringing liquids to a vigorous-hot bubbling and breaking of surface

Braise—After meat has been browned, liquid is added, skillet is covered, and meat is cooked slowly until tender and moist. A good technique for less tender cuts of meet, such as Brisket and Pot Roast.

(to) Bread—To entirely coat a food in bread crumbs, usually by dipping first in flour, second in beaten egg, and lastly in bread crumbs

Bread Knife—A long bladed knife with serrated edges—great for "sawing" rather than "smooching"

Brown—To quickly cook (or vigorously sauté) foods over fairly high heat to brown the surface of the food

Brown Butter—Sautéing butter to a nutty-flavored, golden, deep-brown color—usually with the addition of bread crumbs great over vegetables.

Butterfly—To slice down the center, leaving farthest side intact, and flare open like a butterfly shape, such as "butterflied" shrimp or chicken breasts. Sometimes the sides are folded back up to contain a filling.

Capers—Small salty buds from a bush, usually pickled in a brine. Found in the condiment section or specialty section of your market. Great as a garnish on veal and in salads.

Caramelize—To cook foods until their natural sugars start to turn brown and sweet, such as sautéing onions to deep golden brown and caramelized

Carryover- or Continued- Cooking—The cooking that continues once and item has been removed from its heat source. As it stands (a good example is roast or steak) the food will continue to cook another 5 to 10 degrees. For those who like their meat rare, this can be a significant factor to consider.

Caviar—Salty fish eggs (also called Roe) used for garnish, usually with sour cream and hardboiled egg. The finest caviar comes from Russian sturgeon. Caviar can be an "acquired" taste but adds an elegant garnish to specialty dishes and appetizers.

Chef's Knife—The most versatile knife to have in your kitchen—broad bladed and large, it can tackle just about anything

Chill—To refrigerate a food until it is no longer warm to the touch. Also a comfortable attitude to have in the kitchen, when experimenting with new recipes...

Chop—To cut foods into small pieces, such as chopping an onion

Clarify (butter)—Removing the impurities from butter, by melting it and pouring off the clear, golden liquid into a separate container and discarding the milk solids left behind. Clarified butter can withstand higher temperatures when frying, browning and sautéing, than just regular butter

Coating well—To cover the entire surface with such things as flour, egg-wash and bread crumbs, or a batter, such as Tempura batter.

Cool—To let a food stand at room temperature until it is no longer warm to the touch.

"Comfort foods"—Those dishes we remember as being our favorites—usually not low in calorie content but great in flavor, and should be consumed sensibly

Correcting Seasonings—At end of cooking time, just before serving, take a "taste test" and adjust seasonings and flavors accordingly. This is a good rule to follow, especially for salt, so you don't over-salt the dish. Better to add more salt at the end rather than at the beginning, as foods condense, evaporate and intensify the longer they cook, arriving at many a dish being overly salted.

Crème Fraiche—Cream mixed with buttermilk and left to stand at room temperature until thickened. Can be used in place of sour cream. Crème fraiche can be boiled without the risk of curdling (separating and coagulating)—a nice feature when making sauces.

(to) Cream—To mix foods together to arrive at a smooth, "creamy" consistency

Croutons—Small toasted (and seasoned or not) bread cubes, used usually to garnish salads or make stuffing—a great way to use up old bread

Crushing between fingers—Mashing spices (fresh or dried) to release more flavor before adding to a dish, such as crushing oregano, parsley, etc. while sprinkling into the recipe

De-glaze—To simmer and reduce pan juices to a condensed flavor, usually by adding some wine or broth and picking up all the tasty bits in the bottom of the pan, resulting in a flavorful sauce or gravy

Dice—A finer form of chopping, usually in a more uniform size

Dining—Enjoying a variety of foods, in a relaxed atmosphere, rather than just unconsciously "feeding your face" with the first thing available. Being aware of the satisfying and primary act of enjoying well-prepared food— usually partaken sitting down and with the social company of family and/or friends, without such distractions as TV, reading, "game-boys," phone calls, or political argument, heated discussions, or "food fights."

"Drawn butter"—Unsalted butter that has been clarified (milk solids removed). Usually served in a little warming dish accompanying sea foods, lobster and fish, for dipping.

Dredging—Coating a food with a dry ingredient, such as bread crumbs or flour, before cooking.

(to) Dress—To lightly coat and toss salad greens or vegetables with dressing

Drippings—Liquefied fats and juices left in pan from cooking meats, making a great base for sauces and gravies

Dry Rub—A dry mixture of crushed seasonings, spices and herbs used to enhance flavor of meat by rubbing and pounding the mixture onto the surface of the meat to form a coating before starting the cooking process

Filet (French sp.) or Fillet—A boneless, usually fairly small, premium cut of meat or fish

"Finish"—Swirling in a last-minute pat of butter (in gravies or sauces) to enrich the flavor

Flambé—To finish a recipe, by carefully pouring a warmed portion of liquor into the dish and igniting it—letting the flames burn down before serving, thusly cooking-off the alcohol and leaving only the intense flavor remaining. Never, ever pour alcohol straight from the bottle into the pan! As you are literally holding a bottle-rocket in your hand!

Flash-Frozen—A very quick method of commercially-freezing foods to retain their fresh quality—the next best thing to buying fresh; great for sea foods that can't be kept on ice and gotten to market in a reasonable time.

Flatten or Pound—Tenderizing boneless meat (such as veal cutlets or chicken breasts) by pounding with a mallet or heavy implement until thin and spread out. This breaks down the tough-connective tissues in meat and allows for quicker cooking and sautéing. Meat is made more manageable for adding fillings and rolling up, etc.

Fresh—Never been frozen

Fry—To cook uncovered, in a shallow pan, in hot oil

(French) Fry—To cook in a deeper amount of hot oil

(Deep) Fry—To cook covered with hot oil

Garlic Butter—A mixture of softened butter with minced garlic (or garlic powder)—Great spread and left to melt over grilled or broiled meats (such as unadorned steak or lamb) making a flavorful garnish. (My Father's favorite added touch to his famous sirloin steaks.)

Garlic cloves—The individual pods (or cloves) that make up the whole bulb

Glaze—To cover a food with a glossy finish, such as spooning pan drippings, BBQ sauce, etc. over a meat at end of cooking for an enriched finish

Green Onions—Long thin onions, also known as Scallions, or Spring onions. Use for garnish, and chopped for cooking

Grill—To use you're your skillet like a griddle, such as grilled cheese sandwiches—using a very small amount of fat or cooking spray to prevent sticking

"Hold"—Removing portions of a recipe from the skillet and keeping warm while you finish the dish, make a gravy, etc. The best way to hold food is reserved on a warm platter, "tented" (covered) with foil; or in a warm (200 degree) oven. At some point the held-food can be added back to the dish and warmed thoroughly with remaining ingredients.

Incorporate—To add to, mix, or blend together to make one mixture.

Infuse—To indirectly add flavor by immersing spices (such as bay leaves, peppercorns or garlic cloves) and then removing and discarding at end of cooking. Cutting slits in meat, such as lamb, and inserting peeled garlic cloves to "infuse" flavor throughout the meat.

Julia Child (1912-2004)—The Grande Dame and a pioneer of creative cooking in America, specializing in French Cooking and elegant meals within every cook's reach. Well known for her famous saying "Bon appétit!" and her many exquisitely written cookbooks.

Julienne—To cut foods into slender strips about 1/8-inch thick and matchstick in length.

Lagniappe—A French term for "a little something extra," "an unexpected treat," usually a small gift gratuitously given from a merchant to a customer—like a little chocolate found on your hotel pillow when the bed has been turned down, or an unexpected appetizer or small dessert served as a special treat

Madeira and Marsala—Two fine wines used for drinking and cooking—Often have to go to a fine liquor store to find.

Marinate—Allowing foods to sit and soak in a liquid and seasoning mixture (called "marinade") to help tenderize and make more flavorful before cooking. Discard any leftover, uncooked marinade and definitely do not re-use! For extended marinating, store the item, covered in refrigerator. Plastic baggies or covered- glass containers work the best. Metal containers can have a toxic reaction to the marinade, imparting an undesirable metallic- flavor to the item being marinated.

Mash or Smash (garlic)—Peeling and then mashing garlic cloves under the broad side of a large chef's knife. This releases extra flavor before mincing.

Medallion—Small, round, boneless cut of choice meat (such as Filet Mignon of Beef)

Medley—A representative mixture or grouping of items, such as several vegetables in a dish, or several sea foods cooked together

Mince—To very finely chop into very small dice, such as minced garlic

Mother Sauce—A French nomenclature for the very most basic of sauces—the White Sauce, which can be adapted into a variety of flavored sauces

Oxidation—The discoloration of surfaces on food, such as browning of apple slices and bananas, browning of shredded raw potatoes before cooking. A sprinkling of lemon juice is a good preventative for fruits. Ice water is good for potatoes and vegetables.

Pan or Skillet—Shallow-sided, wide-surfaced, flat-bottomed cooking implement used to cook food, covered or un-covered, utilizing a direct heat source underneath the pan—be it gas flame or electric coil, on the stove top.

(Electric) Fry Pan or (Electric) Skillet—the heat source is built right into the bottom of the pan, utilizing a temperature dial on the side to accurately control over-all heat, in bottom of pan.

Palate—A range of culinary tastes

Palette—A range of artistic values and qualities

Pan juices—the resultant, flavorful juices remaining in the skillet after cooking, making a flavorful base for additional sauce or gravy

Pare—To peel and trim with a small, flexible kitchen knife (thus the name paring knife)

Parboil—Partially cooking in boiling liquid, usually to tenderize or prepare for a further cooking process

Port—A sweet Portuguese drinking wine that can add rich flavor to a dish, especially stews and pot roast

Red Onions-Great, sliced into rings for salads, also known as Spanish Onions

Reduce—To cook pan-liquids and juices, uncovered, to thicken and condense into a sauce or gravy with maximum flavor at final stage of cooking

Render—To remove, melt, sear, or parboil fat from a piece of meat

Re-constitute, Macerate, or Plump—To bring back the original consistency of a dried food by soaking and standing in liquid—such as "reconstituting" sun-dried tomatoes, dried chilies, dried specialty mushrooms and dried fruits.

(A good example is raisins "plumped" in liquid; or raisins "macerated" in rum for an additional flavor.)

Saffron (threads or powder)—A very expensive, exotic spice (made from the stigmas of crocus flowers) that imparts beautiful color and flavor to such dishes as Paella and other rice-inclusive dishes. A little bit goes a long way. Comes in thread-form or crushed powder. You may have to go to a specialty store to find it.

Sauté—To quickly (but delicately) cook foods, uncovered in a shallow pan or skillet until browned, using a small amount of butter, oil, or fat

Scallions—Long thin onions, also known as green onions—not to be confused with shallots

Sear—Browning meats quickly, on all sides, over high heat to seal in juices before further cooking

Shallow Pan Method for Deep Frying—Setting your skillet on very high temperature with a depth of ¼ inch to ½ inch of hot oil, to mimic using a deep-fryer, for such dishes as Tempura Shrimp, French Fried Shrimp, Rosettes and Donuts

Shallots—Small purplish bulbs, yielding a delicate flavor between onion and garlic. Usually used in minced form, when onion or garlic would be too overpowering in flavor

Sherry—An excellent, rich wine with which to flavor sauces

Shiitakes, Portabellas, Chanterelles, Straw Mushrooms—Specialty mushrooms found in markets today that take us far beyond the common white, button mushroom

Simmer—To slowly cook, usually covered, in liquid just below boiling point

Stir-fry—Quickly frying food in a small amount of hot oil, stirring and tossing all the while

Stock, Broth, or Bouillon—A highly flavored, strained liquid containing the extracted flavor of a meat or vegetable, from extended cooking. Originally made from boiling from scratch, we now have the convenience of canned, crystals or cubes.

(to)Sweat—Cooking over low or moderate heat to soften but not brown—such as gently cooking diced onion until it "sweats" and softens, but doesn't change color

"Tent"—To cover with a dome of cooking foil before adding cover to pan, thus "double-covering" the food for moister cooking and re-circulation of steam and pan-juices.

Thicken—To cause a liquid to become more dense by adding (in the case of gravies and sauces) flour or cornstarch, mixed in a little additional liquid themselves, to "thicken" pan juices into gravy or sauce This is done over moderate heat, stirring all the while, until you arrive at the consistency you desire.

Toast—Browning foods (such as nuts and croutons) with the use of dry heat—either by stirring in a dry pan, or baking on a dry cookie sheet in the oven.

Toss—We all know how to toss a salad, but it can also be important to gently mix (by "tossing") meat mixtures when making meatloaf and meatballs. This keeps the mixture from getting dense and tough through overworking and heavy-handed mixing.

Vinaigrette—A blend of oil, vinegar (or lemon juice) and seasonings to be used as a salad dressing, or in some cases as a marinade.

Water bath—A shallow pan of simmering water used to surround a second pan in which food is being gently cooked. Often used a substitute for double-boiler cooking.

Well-balanced—The precise taste of all your spices and seasonings coming together in one succulent flavor, none overpowering the other—yet at the same time, all seasonings remain identifiable

White pepper—Find in the spice section of your market. Use in place of black pepper when seasoning white sauces and light colored dishes.

Zest—The intensely flavored and aromatic outer peel of citrus fruit, used to add or augment citrus flavor in dishes. Usually grated very fine, not including any pithy portion just under the peel.

Other Books by WENDY LOUISE

The Complete Crockery Cookbook:
Create Spectacular Meals with Your Slow Cooker

The resurgence of the slow cooker has provided many families with the means to recreate the family dinner hour in their home. Now, you too can join the ranks of those enjoying hearty and homey dinners by simply using this long-overlooked kitchen asset!

What's more, slow cookers aren't just for soups, stews and roasts. Wendy Louise has taken desserts, meals for entertaining, nutritious side dishes, along with every day fare, and adapted them to carefree crockery classics.

A special section shows you how to convert "family heirloom" recipes into spectacular slow-cooking favorites. Filled with anecdotes, *Cook's Notes* and *Tips from the Kitchen*, over 180 recipes bring a creative flair to crockery cooking!

6 x 9 - Trade Paper - 232 pages - $16.00 US/$22.95 CAN
ISBN: 1-891400-29-0

Brook Noel with Wendy Louise

Rush Hour Recipes

Recipes, Tips and Wisdom for Every Day Of The Year

Easy and simple mealtime solutions are within reach of every busy family with the Rush Hour Cook's late st collection. Each day of the year features a new recipe along with a personal challenge, kitchen tip or words of wisdom.

For those who want to reduce their grocery bills, save time, and enjoy incredibly delicious recipes with simple ingredients, the Rush Hour Cook will become a one-stop solution. Like all of the books in the Rush Hour Series, this ultimate collection follows the five Rush Hour Rules:

· All ingredients are pronounceable through the phonetic use of the English language.

· Each ingredient can be found in the market without engaging in a full scale scavenger hunt.

· No list of ingredients shall be longer than the instructions.

· Each recipe has to be durable enough to survive the "Queen-of-Incapable-Cooking."

· The Rush Hour Cook's finicky child will eat it – or some portion of it.

288 pages • 8.5 by 11 • ISBN 1-891400-67-3 • $22.95/C$32.95

Other Cookbooks from CHAMPION PRESS, LTD.

Basil to Thyme
Culinary Endeavors from the
Garden to the Kitchen
By Tim Haas and Jan Beane

Two of America's most loved
pastimes, cooking and gardening,
come together in this delightful
collection of recipes.

Spiral Bound: $22.95 US

Crazy About Crockery!
101 Easy and Inexpensive
Recipes for Less than 75 cents
a Serving

In this collection, cookbook
author Penny E. Stone brings 101
of her family's classic slow
cooker favorites to your kitchen—
all for less than 75 cents per
serving.

Trade Paperback $12 US

Power Desserts:
The Ultimate Collection of Reduced-Fat,
Nutrient-Packed Indulgences
KAREN PELLEGRIN

ISBN: 1-891400-65-8 $12/95 US

These easy-to-prepare desserts are power-packed with nutrients while reduced in fat. Learn about the components of a healthy diet and power-baking while preparing cookies, brownies, cakes, pies, muffins, and cheesecakes.

The Rush Hour Cook's
Weekly Wonders:
19 Weekly Meal Plans Complete with Shopping Lists for
Today's Busy Family
BROOK NOEL

Featuring 19 quick and easy weekly menu plans with shopping lists, The Rush Hour Cook offers proven quick and easy dinner solutions.

ISBN 1-8914-00-14-2 $16

CHAMPION PRESS LTD.

**Visit www.championpress.com
to sign up for our free cooking updates,
download recipes, read book excerpts and more.**

To order our products please download an order form at
www.championpress.com
or call 877-250-3354
(toll free)